RODALE'S
SUCCESSFUL ORGANIC GARDENING™
IMPROVING
THE SOIL

RODALE'S
SUCCESSFUL ORGANIC GARDENING™
IMPROVING
THE SOIL

ERIN HYNES

Rodale Press, Emmaus, Pennsylvania

Copyright © 1994 by Weldon Russell Pty Ltd

All rights reserved. No part of this publication may be reproduced or
transmitted in any form or by any means, electronic or mechanical,
including photocopy, recording, or any other storage and retrieval
system, without the written permission of the publisher.

If you have any questions or comments concerning this book,
please write to:

Rodale Press
Book Readers' Service
33 East Minor Street
Emmaus, PA 18098

Library of Congress Cataloging-in-Publication Data

Hynes, Erin.
    Improving the soil / Erin Hynes
        p.   cm. — (Rodale's successful organic gardening)
    Includes index.
    ISBN 0–87596–617–9 hardcover — ISBN 0–87596–618–7
paperback
        1. Garden soils. 2. Organic gardening. 3. Soil management.
I. Title. II. Series.
S596.75.H95 1994
631.4—dc20   94–375
                                                 CIP

Produced by Mandarin Offset, Hong Kong
Printed in Hong Kong on acid-free paper ∞

Rodale Press Staff:
    Executive Editor: Margaret Lydic Balitas
    Managing Editor: Barbara W. Ellis
    Editor: Nancy J. Ondra
    Copy Editor: Carolyn R. Mandarano

Produced for Rodale Press by Weldon Russell Pty Ltd
107 Union Street, North Sydney NSW 2060, Australia
a member of the Weldon International Group of Companies

    Publisher: Elaine Russell
    General Manager: Susan Hurley
    Managing Editor: Ariana Klepac
    Project Coordinator: Libby Frederico
    Horticultural Consultant: Cheryl Maddocks
    Copy Editor: Yani Silvana
    Designer: Rowena Sheppard
    Picture Researcher: Anne Ferrier
    Illustrators: Barbara Rodanska, Jan Smith
    Macintosh Layout Artist: Silvia Martello
    Indexer: Michael Wyatt
    Production Manager: Dianne Leddy

A KEVIN WELDON PRODUCTION

Distributed in the book trade by St. Martin's Press

2 4 6 8 10 9 7 5 3 1 hardcover
2 4 6 8 10 9 7 5 3 1 paperback

Opposite: Japanese maple *(Acer japonicum)*
Half title: Lettuces
Opposite title page: *Delphinium* 'Shimmer'
Title page: *Dahlia pinnata*
Opposite contents: Kohlrabi
Contents: *Zinnia elegans* (bottom)
Back cover: *Rosa rugosa* (bottom)

CONTENTS

INTRODUCTION

It's not surprising that most people don't care much about soil. After all, it's pretty easy to take soil for granted—it's just *there,* quietly being red or brown or gray or black. We notice the soil if a windstorm whips it in our eyes or someone tracks it through the house, but most of the time we're much more inclined to notice the wide variety of plants that adorn the soil than the soil itself.

But good gardeners realize that the soil has a tremendous effect on the plants that grow in it. After all, plants get most of what they need to grow—including support, water, nutrients, warmth, and oxygen—from the soil. Some soils are better at providing those things than others. How good a job they do depends on a variety of complex and intertwined factors, including the kind of rock the soil developed from, the organisms that live there, and how big the individual grains of soil are and how well they stick together.

Even though soils are complex, you don't have to be a soil scientist to grow great-tasting tomatoes or beautiful petunias. You can learn a lot about your soil just by looking at it, touching it, and growing things in it. To learn things that seeing and touching can't reveal, you can perform simple home tests or have a laboratory test your soil for you. All the information you gather will help you make decisions about planting, watering, fertilizing, mulching, and many other seemingly unrelated aspects of gardening.

If you are one of the few gardeners that has naturally fertile, loose, healthy soil, congratulations! Now, make sure you *keep* your soil in good shape by working it properly and maintaining the right level of organic matter. If your soil is less than perfect, don't despair: Each time you dig, plant, or mulch you have the chance to compensate for the problems and build better soil. No matter what kind of soil you are starting with, *Rodale's Successful Organic Gardening: Improving the Soil* will guide you through the process of developing the best possible growing conditions and keeping your soil healthy and productive for years to come.

Choosing plants that are adapted to your soil conditions is the key to a successful garden. Azaleas, for instance, put on a splendid spring show in acid, humus-rich soil; they would be weak and spindly on a site with dry, alkaline soil.

HOW TO USE THIS BOOK

Successful gardening starts with the soil. Without healthy soil, you can't grow healthy plants. Unfortunately, the soil is often overlooked, taken for granted, or abused. It's dug when it's too wet, leading to clods and compaction, or tilled to a fine powder, increasing the chance of erosion. Then it's blamed for being too heavy, too dry, or too clumpy. If you understand the characteristics of the soil you're starting with, and take care of it with those characteristics in mind, you'll be well on your way to developing a great garden.

Rodale's Successful Organic Gardening: Improving the Soil is your guide to getting the most from your soil by caring for it with organic gardening methods. It shows you how to learn what kind of soil you have, how to make it better, and how to get it to produce healthy plants—whether you're growing vegetables, flowers, woody plants, lawns, fruit, or plants in containers.

Developing great soil begins with knowing what you have to work with. In "Understanding Your Soil," starting on page 12, you'll find out how to take a close look at your soil. The chapter explains how soils develop and what they're made of. You'll learn about the importance of soil texture and structure and how these characteristics affect the plants you want to grow. "Understanding Your Soil" introduces the concept of soil nutrients and tells how pH—acidity and alkalinity—determines whether or not your plants can use the nutrients that are already there. You'll learn how your soil's color is a clue to its characteristics and find tips on taking soil tests to get details your senses can't give you.

Healthy populations of worms, fungi, and other soil organisms are essential for a healthy organic garden. The creatures that inhabit the soil, both visible and microscopic, are the topic of "Life in the Soil," starting on page 24. This chapter tells how you can encourage these helpful subterranean dwellers. It also shows how plant roots play an important part in the soil and discusses both beneficial and harmful soil insects, as well as beneficial and disease-causing soil microorganisms.

Adding organic matter is undoubtedly the most important step you can take in developing great garden soil. In "Building Soil Organic Matter," starting on page 40, you'll discover why organic matter is so important and learn about the various ways you can add it to your garden. Compost is one of the best sources of organic matter, and you'll find out how you can make your own compost by recycling garden and kitchen wastes. This chapter includes a discussion of mulch and how it can suppress weeds, conserve water, and add organic matter to the soil. It also tells how to use cover crops and green manures to improve soil.

As plants grow, they draw nutrients from the soil. You need to replace the ones your crops remove and make up for those that the soil naturally lacks. Starting on page 70, "Understanding Fertilizers" explains what nutrients plants need, in what amounts, and what role they play in plant growth. You'll learn what deficiency symptoms to look for. You'll also discover the ins and outs of buying and applying organic fertilizers.

If you're like most gardeners, there's at least one thing you'd like to change about your soil. "Dealing with Problem Soil," starting on page 96, gets down to the tough gardening challenges: slopes, poor drainage, excessive acidity and alkalinity, high levels of salt, too much sand and clay, rockiness, and compacted soil. Some of the solutions are surprisingly easy and inexpensive, others are more complicated and expensive. This chapter also looks at plant diseases that live in the soil and what you can do about them.

The right tools can help you do any job faster.

"Cultivating the Soil," starting on page 116, explains how to know when the soil is ready to dig and what tools you can use to cultivate it. You'll also discover tips for buying and maintaining your tools and for digging properly to avoid an aching back.

Of course, the whole point of understanding and improving your soil is to be able to grow great plants. In "Soil Care for Your Plants," starting on page 136, you'll learn how to help your soil meet the needs of different kinds of plants—vegetables and herbs; flowers; trees, shrubs, and vines; lawns and groundcovers; fruiting crops; and containers and houseplants. You'll find out how to prepare planting sites, fertilize and mulch, and maintain healthy soil to have the best garden ever.

Encyclopedic Guides

Some of the chapters in *Rodale's Successful Organic Gardening: Improving the Soil* are followed by guides that tell you more about plants, organisms, and materials mentioned in the main part of the chapter. Starting on page 32, the "Guide to Soil Life" tells you what specific insects and other organisms do for your soil. Use the photographs and descriptions to help you identify the small things that live in your garden. "Organic Mulches," starting on page 52, describes 15 common organic mulches and their good and bad points. It also tells how to use them and where to get them, and it includes photographs so you know what they look like. On page 62, the "Cover Crops and Green Manures" gives specifics about growing 15 different crops as green manures—when to plant, when to turn them under, and what they'll do for the soil.

In "Organic Fertilizers and Amendments," starting on page 86, you'll find photographs of 19 different fertilizers and information on what each fertilizer is, what it does, how to apply it, and where you can find it. "Soil-working Tools," starting on page 128, tells you how to buy, use, and care for more than a dozen tools.

These guides are designed to tell you what you need to know about a variety of soil-related topics. The diagram below is a sample of one of these practical pages.

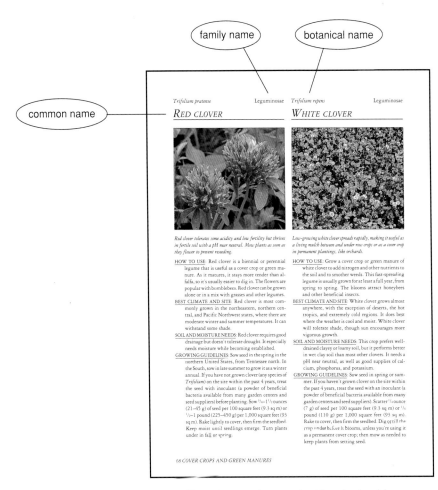

Sample page from a plant by plant guide.

UNDERSTANDING YOUR SOIL

In war and sports, the adage is, "Know thy enemy." In gardening, it's "Know thy soil." Few soils are unconquerable foes, but almost all of them have at least one flaw that makes peaceful coexistence difficult. Soils can be too thin, too rocky, too clayey, too porous, too acid, too alkaline, too high in one mineral, too low in another—almost every soil is too something. Fortunately, virtually any soil can be dramatically improved with some time and effort. Getting to know your soil's characteristics will help you choose the right techniques for dealing with it successfully. And when your soil is in good shape, your whole garden will naturally be healthier and more beautiful.

If you're new to gardening, you may look at your soil and wonder what there is to know. Don't fall victim to the dirt-is-dirt syndrome. As experienced gardeners know—especially those who have gardened in different regions—soil is complex beneath its unassuming demeanor. It can be sandy, silty, or clayey; loose and crumbly or as hard as concrete; dry, moist, or waterlogged. Soil also contains dozens of chemical elements, in varying amounts and combinations.

In this chapter, you'll learn how these and other characteristics affect the plants you want to grow. "What Is Soil?" on page 14 will give you a thorough grounding in soil basics—what it's made of, where it comes from, and how it forms. "Getting a Feel for Texture" on page 16 can help you figure out if your soil is primarily sand, clay, or that elusive "loam" that so many gardeners wish for. In "Understanding Soil Structure" on page 18, you'll learn how to tell what kind of structure your garden soil has and how to improve a soil with poor structure so all of your plants will grow better. "Knowing about Nutrients and pH" on page 20 tells about the different elements your plants can get from the soil and explains how factors like acidity or alkalinity can affect plant growth. "Taking a Look at Soil Color" on page 22 will give you some insight into learning the characteristics of your soil just by looking at it. And if you really want to know the "dirt" on your soil, follow the simple step-by-step guidelines in "Taking Soil Tests" on page 23 to find out how to collect and prepare soil samples for professional testing.

Soil may all look the same to you, but your plants can tell the difference! Understanding the various properties of your soil will help you pick the best-adapted plants and give them the right conditions for strong, healthy growth.

What Is Soil?

Just as the air you breathe is actually a mixture of different gases, your garden soil is a mixture of solids, spaces, and living organisms. About 97 percent of the solid part of soil is old rock that's been broken down into tiny particles over millions of years. The remaining 3 percent or so is organic matter, made up of decomposed plant and animal tissue. Intermingled with these bits of rock and organic matter is an equal volume of space, filled with air and water.

This mixture of minerals, organic matter, air, and water can support a diverse population of living organisms, from algae and fungi to earthworms and moles. Most important to you as a gardener is that soil is a habitat for roots, providing the physical support, nutrients, and water that your plants need to grow and thrive. Maintaining the right balance of minerals, organic matter, air, and water is the goal of good soil management.

Look at Your Soil Layers

In nature, soils tend to all share the same basic ingredients, but they can vary in thousands of ways. Each soil has its own set of characteristics—including color, texture, structure, depth, fertility, and drainage—that makes it different from all other soils. Fortunately, you don't need to know everything there is to know about soil to develop a healthy, productive garden. But it is important to realize that not all soil management techniques will work for all kinds of soil. Understanding the characteristics of the soils on your property will help you choose the best practices for your conditions and plants.

Start your investigation by looking under the soil surface. Dig a hole about 2 to 3 feet (60 to 90 cm) deep, if possible, and look at the soil layers. This cross section of the soil (called its profile) will probably show a layer of dark, crumbly soil on the top. This topsoil

Where Soil Comes From

How can soil be different from place to place? It's due to the influence of five natural factors: climate, living organisms, parent material, topography, and time. These factors affect how fast a soil forms and ages and what the soil is like.

Climate Soil begins to form when wind and rain wear away at a mass of rock—the soil's parent material. Soil develops faster in warm climates than in cold and in wet regions than in dry.

Living organisms Animals and living plants loosen the soil and add organic matter with their excretions and dropped leaves. Microorganisms decompose dead plants and animals, releasing nutrients and organic matter. Human activity (especially gardening) can also have a great impact on the soil at a given site.

Parent material The parent material helps determine whether your soil is sandy or high in clay. Sandstones, for instance, weather into sandy soils, while fine-particled shales tend to produce clayey soil. The parent material also influences whether the soil is acid or alkaline and what kinds of nutrients are present. Limestone, for example, tends to form soil that has a neutral or alkaline

pH, while granite yields more acid soils.

Topography Soils on flat land or in low areas are often deeper than those on hills, since water carries soil down slopes and deposits it at the base. Slopes protected by some kind of groundcover tend to be less eroded than bare-soil slopes.

Time When people are involved, soil characteristics can change in a matter of days, weeks, or months. But most soil-forming factors—climate, soil organisms, parent material, and topography—act over millions of years. Since biological activity is very slow in cold or dry conditions, polar regions and deserts tend to have "young," rocky soils with thin topsoil and little organic matter. Tropical regions have "old" soils. Eons of rain have washed away nutrients, and the warm temperatures have encouraged active soil organisms to deplete the organic matter. Temperate areas with moderate temperatures and rainfall form soils of varying depth and fertility.

Soil forms many layers as it ages. The top layer tends to be darker and richer in organic matter than lower layers.

Moles, gophers, and other creatures loosen and mix the soil as they burrow below the surface.

is rich in the organic matter left by dead and decaying plants. The top layer is deeper in regions where deep-rooted prairie grasses once grew and where cooler temperatures slow the breakdown of organic matter. In other areas, the topsoil is often much thinner. Dry climates support fewer plants, so there's less organic matter overall, while warm and wet conditions speed decomposition, depleting organic matter faster. Sites around new construction also may have little or no topsoil.

Below the topsoil is the subsoil, which may have several layers. Little organic matter reaches the subsoil; what does reach it is clay that washes down from the layer above. A loose,

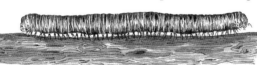

Millipedes, bacteria, and other soil organisms play an important role in breaking down dead plant material in soil.

sandy subsoil allows for good water drainage and encourages deep rooting; tight, clayey subsoil may produce waterlogged conditions and impede root growth. Unlike topsoil, which is relatively easy to change, the subsoil is difficult to modify. If your subsoil is poor, or if you have no topsoil at all, your challenge is to build soil organic matter levels as quickly as possible. For more information, see "Building Soil Organic Matter," starting on page 41.

As you examine the soil, take the time to learn about some of its other characteristics, like the texture, structure, and color. (You'll find more information on these topics in "Getting a Feel for Texture" on page 16; "Understanding Soil Structure" on page 18; and "Taking a Look at Soil Color" on page 22.) As you learn about your soil, jot down your observations in a notebook for easy reference.

Even on a single site, the various soil layers can have dramatically different characteristics. A rich, loamy topsoil can develop over a hard-packed, nutrient-poor layer; a loose, easy-to-dig layer can give way to hard rock just a few feet down. Exploring the soil below the surface can clue you in to these otherwise hidden problems.

With good management, even poor subsoil can produce good crops.

Loose, gravelly soil is ideal for plants that need good drainage.

Well-prepared, humus-rich soil will support many kinds of plants.

Getting a Feel for Texture

As rock breaks down into soil, it forms progressively smaller pieces of various sizes. The smallest of these pieces (those 2 mm or less in diameter) are called soil particles. (The larger pieces are usually called gravel or stone—or other, less-technical terms by frustrated gardeners.) Scientists classify soil particles into three different groups—sand, silt, and clay—depending on the size. The relative percentages of sand, silt, and clay determine the texture of your soil. They also affect important soil characteristics like drainage and nutrient availability, which in turn influence how well your plants will grow.

Understanding Sand, Clay, and Silt

Of the three types of soil particles, sand is the largest. A grain of sand can be as fine as 0.05 mm or as coarse as 2 mm—about the size of the period at the end of this sentence. (Bigger than that, it's considered gravel.) Microscopic silt particles range from 0.0002 mm up to 0.05 mm. And tinier clay particles are less than 0.002 mm in diameter; you'd need an electron microscope to see these.

Sand   Sand particles are large and often irregularly shaped, so they don't fit closely together. Water drains quickly between them. Dissolved nutrients tend to drain out with the water, making sandy soils relatively infertile. Sandy soils are often described as being light because they're easy to dig.

Clay   Clay particles, on the other hand, are small and flat; they pack so closely that water has trouble draining between them. Nutrients don't drain away readily, but roots may have a hard time growing between the tightly packed particles to reach the nutrients there. Clayey soils are sticky and heavy when wet and hard when dry. In either condition, they are difficult to dig. They are also slow to warm up in spring.

Silt   Intermediate-sized silt particles are irregularly

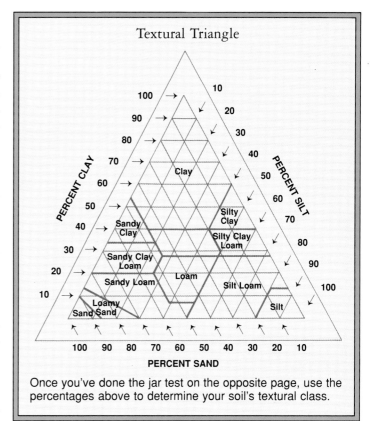

Textural Triangle

Once you've done the jar test on the opposite page, use the percentages above to determine your soil's textural class.

shaped like sand, but they are often coated with a thin layer of clay. As a result, they tend to have some characteristics of both sand and clay.

What Class is Your Soil In?

Few soils are all sand or clay or silt—most are a combination. Loam is often described as the "ideal" garden soil—dark, fertile, and high in organic matter. Actually, though, a loam isn't necessarily any of those things. Technically, loam is a balanced mixture of about 40 percent sand, 40 percent silt, and 20 percent clay. It may be any color and can have lots of organic matter or almost none at all. A loamy soil holds usable amounts of water and nutrients but drains well, providing good growing conditions for many different types of plants.

Fortunately, having a loamy soil is certainly not a requirement for a good garden. With careful management,

Sandy soil tends to be dry and low in nutrients.

Clayey soil can be sticky when wet and hard when dry.

Silty soil is fine and powdery and can pack like clay.

Loamy soil has a balance of sand, silt, and clay particles.

How do you know what class your soil fits into? Only a laboratory test can tell you the exact percentage of each particle type in a soil sample. But you can get a fairly accurate estimate by trying one of the simple home tests below.

The feel test To see how clayey your soil is, rub a moistened ball of soil about the size of a grape between your palms. The goal is to make a "worm" or rope. If you succeed, your soil is more than 15 percent clay; the longer the worm, the higher the percent of clay.

To check for sand, place a chunk of soil in your palm and wet it enough to form a small puddle. Rub a finger in it: If it's gritty, your soil is sandy; if it's smooth, your soil is silty.

The jar test A more scientific method is based on the fact that big particles settle out of water faster than little ones.

You'll need a cup of air-dried soil collected from different places in the garden; a clean, fairly narrow glass jar with a tight-fitting lid; distilled water; a grease pencil or masking tape to mark the jar; and a teaspoon of nonsudsing dishwasher detergent. (If your soil is high in lime, use baking soda instead of detergent. To check for lime, mix a teaspoon of vinegar with a teaspoon of soil. If it fizzes, use baking soda.)

Crush the soil with a rolling pin or give it a whirl in an old food processor (one that you no longer use for food). Pick out any stones, sticks, or leaves. Place the soil in the jar, add the detergent, fill the jar two-thirds full of water, and close the jar tightly. Shake the jar vigorously for a minute or two, then set it down in an out-of-the-way spot.

A minute after you set the jar down, the sand settles out. Mark the soil level with the grease pencil or masking tape—this is level A. Wait 2 hours for the silt to settle, then mark the new soil level—this is level B. Let the jar rest for a few days, until the clay settles, then mark the new soil level (level C). Measure the height of each level from the bottom of the jar.

Use these formulas to figure out the percentages of sand, silt, and clay:

Percent sand = (A/C) x 100

Percent silt = [(B-A)/C] x 100

Percent clay = [(C-B)/C] x 100

Use the triangle on the opposite page to see how these percentages relate to your soil's textural class.

---

you can develop loose, moisture-holding, nutrient-rich conditions. Besides sand, silt, clay, and loam, there are eight other soil textural classes your soil could fit into; their names indicate which particles dominate. A sand with a bit of silt and/or clay is a loamy sand; add more silt or clay and it becomes sandy loam. Toss in even more clay and you have sandy clay loam. Other soil textural classes are sandy clay, silty clay, silty clay loam, silt loam, and clay loam.

Knowing the relative texture of your soil will help you predict how well it drains and what plants will grow there. "Try a Simple Texture Test" will tell you how to get an estimate of your soil's textural class. If your soil is high in sand, read "Managing Sandy Soil" on page 108. To find out more about handling soils that are high in clay, see "Caring for Clayey Soil" on page 110.

Working clayey soil when it's wet produces lumps that dry to hard clods. Adding organic matter will loosen heavy soil.

It's worth a little effort to develop and protect a good, granular soil structure; your plants will thank you for it!

Soil Structure Helpers

You have allies in your battle for good soil structure—the small creatures that crawl through your soil. Earthworms are perhaps the most famous soil builders. Their tunneling loosens and aerates tight soil, and the organic matter they drag down encourages stable soil granules. Rodents churn the soil as they dig and mix organic matter into the subsoil. Plant roots also improve soil structure by adding organic matter below the surface as they break down. Plus, the tiny passages left by the decayed roots allow water and air easier access to lower soil layers, in turn encouraging even better microorganism and plant growth.

Understanding Soil Structure

While texture refers to the types and amounts of mineral particles in your soil, the structure tells how those particles clump together. Developing and maintaining good structure is one of the most important parts of building healthy soil.

The ideal soil for most plants is made up of small, soft granules or crumbs, less than $1/2$ inch (1 cm) in diameter. Soil with this loose, granular structure is said to have good tilth. Soil with good tilth is easy to dig. Plus, the crumbs are small enough to make good contact with seeds and roots, so the water and nutrients the plants need are close enough to be absorbed.

Not all soils have this ideal structure. Some, in fact, are structureless. They may be single grained, which means that the individual particles aren't joined at all, letting water and nutrients flow through quickly. Or soils may be massive, meaning that the particles pack together in tight, irregular clods. These clods can block developing roots, and the spaces between the clods may be big enough to create air pockets where roots dry out.

With good care, even poor soil can produce great results.

Some soils just naturally develop with poor structure. Others may have been damaged by poor gardening practices. Working the soil when it's too wet (especially if it's on the clayey side) can lead to large clods that harden when they dry. Walking over it too often causes compaction, leaving less room for water and air. Working the ground often—especially with a soil-pulverizing rotary tiller—can turn crumbly, granular soil into a structureless powder.

Building and Maintaining Good Structure

Because the roots of most plants—annual flowers, lawn grass, vegetables, and herbs—grow mainly in the topsoil, it's the structure of this layer that should concern you most. Fortunately, this layer of soil is also the easiest one to improve.

Before you start digging, wait until the soil has dried out a bit; otherwise, you can ruin the soil structure.

"Blocky" structure is common in the subsoil in humid regions.

Soils that form from glacial or river materials often have platy structure.

Structureless soil that is tightly compacted can lead to poor drainage.

While it's seldom possible to change your soil's texture (short of adding tons of sand, silt, or clay), you can have a great effect on soil structure. The real key to building great garden soil is adding ample amounts of organic matter, in the form of materials like compost, manure, grass clippings, or chopped leaves. As earthworms and other organisms break down organic matter into stable humus, they release sticky gums that help bind soil particles together into granules. The humus itself is light and fluffy, helping to loosen up tight, compacted soil.

Once you have soil with good structure, take care of it. Avoid working soil when it is too wet or too dry. Dig in your garden only when a fistful of soil holds together loosely when you open your hand, then crumbles when you touch it. Work the soil as infrequently as possible—perhaps once a year—and dig in more organic matter when you do. To avoid compacting the soil, don't tromp on it when it's wet, and reroute foot traffic away from planted areas. If you must step into garden beds, lay boards across the area and use those to walk on to spread out your weight over the soil and minimize compaction.

Structure below the Surface

While it's relatively easy to develop good soil structure at the surface, you have much less influence over the subsoil. There, the parent material plays a greater role in determining how the particles group themselves.

Next time you dig a deep hole, take a look at the structure of the deepest soil you can see. Observe the soil in place on the side of the hole, or break off a hand-sized piece. Loose, structureless subsoil may allow water and nutrients to drain away from roots too quickly, leading to droughty conditions at the surface. A tight, massive subsoil will interfere with the drainage of excess water, usually leading to waterlogged conditions.

While granules are fairly uncommon in the subsoil, you may see other kinds of structures there. In uncultivated soils, or those laid down by water or ice (along rivers and streams or in glacial areas), particles often arrange themselves in flat sheets, called plates. In dry regions, you're likely to see vertical columns that may be 6 inches (15 cm) or more in diameter and of varying lengths. In humid regions, the subsoil is usually made up of angular or slightly rounded cubes that range in size from less than 1 inch (2.5 cm) wide to 2 inches (5 cm) wide or more.

Tight, platy soil can discourage growth.

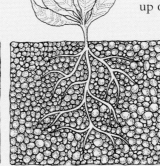

Roots grow easily in granular soil.

Your plants need a balanced supply of many different nutrients to produce healthy growth and high yields.

Knowing about Nutrients and pH

You may know gardeners in your neighborhood who grow beautiful flowers, tasty vegetables, and bushels of fruit without worrying much about soil nutrients. They may scatter a few handfuls of commercial fertilizer around their petunias or water their tomatoes every few weeks with a liquid fertilizer and be happy with the results. So why should you care about what nutrients your own soil has to offer your plants?

Knowing the natural fertility level of your soil will allow you to identify and correct any deficiencies, so the nutrients will be there as your plants need them. Monitoring soil pH will help you choose the best-

Root crops such as potatoes and beets need a soil with balanced amounts of nitrogen, phosphorus, and potassium.

adapted plants for your site and let you keep the pH at the optimum level for those plants. If you want the brightest flowers, the highest yields, and the healthiest plants, it's definitely worth spending a few minutes to learn about soil nutrients.

Understanding Soil Nutrients

As your plants grow, they take in radiant energy from the sun and convert it to chemical energy. This chemical energy is stored in the leaves, stems, fruits, seeds, and roots, providing a major source of food for people, other animals, and some insects. Producing this energy takes lots of carbon, hydrogen, and oxygen (from air and water), plus smaller amounts of mineral elements from the soil.

The essential elements that your plants draw from the soil are commonly referred to as nutrients. Plants use relatively large amounts of nitrogen, phosphorus, potassium, calcium, magnesium, and sulfur. These elements are referred to as macronutrients. Micro-nutrients—including iron, manganese, boron, molybdenum, copper, zinc, chlorine, and nickel—are used in much smaller quantities, but your plants still need them for plant growth.

Nutrients may come from many sources. Some essential minerals are liberated as rocks break down into soil. Organic matter also releases nutrients as it decomposes into humus. And you may add nutrients by applying supplemental fertilizers to the garden. "Understanding Fertilizers," starting on page 71, covers in more detail the role of nutrients in your plants and the different ways you can boost natural soil nutrient levels.

Try a Litmus Test

A litmus test is an easy and inexpensive way to get a rough idea of your soil's acidity or alkalinity. You'll need litmus paper, which you can buy at a garden center or scientific-supply store; a clean container; distilled water; and about a tablespoon of soil.

1. Put the soil in the clean container.

2. Stir in distilled water until the mixture is the consistency of a milkshake.

3. Let it stand an hour; if it gets too thick, add a little more water.

4. Place a strip of litmus paper in the soil-water mixture and leave it in for at least 60 seconds.

5. Remove the paper and rinse it with distilled water.

6. Match the color of the paper to the chart that came with the kit.

Making Sense of Soil pH

Having the right amount and balance of nutrients in your soil is just part of developing good soil fertility: The nutrients must also be available to plant roots. And that's where pH comes in.

First, let's review a bit of chemistry. Remember that the pH of any liquid—water, soda pop, dish detergent—is a measure of how acid or alkaline it is. The pH scale goes from 1 through 14, with 1 being most acid, 14 being most alkaline, and 7 being neutral. Each number represents a tenfold change in acidity or alkalinity. For example, a liquid with a pH of 5 is ten times more acid than one with a pH of 6.

At different pH levels, the elements in your soil will form different chemical compounds. Some of these compounds will dissolve in water (so they are soluble); some compounds are insoluble. Since nutrients must dissolve in water to be accessible to plants, your plants can't take up nutrients in insoluble compounds.

Most essential nutrients form soluble compounds when the pH is around 6.5 to 7.0. That's why most plants grow best in this pH range. (Soil organisms, like earthworms and beneficial bacteria, also prefer a soil pH between 6 and 8.) As the pH goes down (becomes more acid), nutrients like phosphorus, calcium, and magnesium become less available. At higher

It's worth a few minutes to take a soil test, especially before putting in permanent plantings, like fruit trees.

(more alkaline) pH levels, elements like iron and manganese are much less soluble.

Of course, not all plants need the same pH. Some, like blueberries, rhododendrons, and azaleas, tend to grow best in acid soil (with a pH around 4.5 to 5.5). Others, like cabbages and baby's-breath, can thrive with a pH on the alkaline side. If you know your soil's pH, you can choose the plants that are best adapted to your garden's natural conditions. Or you may try to adjust the pH to fit the plants you want to grow.

Finding Out about Your Soil's Fertility

Garden centers sell litmus paper and pH test kits, which you can use to get a rough idea of your soil's pH (see "Try a Litmus Test" for more details). Their accuracy varies with the test's sensitivity and the user's skill. The surest approach is to have a soil-testing lab analyze your soil. Depending on the results, you may want to read "Gardening in Acid Soil" on page 102 or "Growing in Alkaline Soil" on page 104 to find management tips for your particular garden conditions.

You can also buy home test kits to measure soil fertility, but they may not give reliable results. Again, you'll get the most dependable readings from a professional soil analysis. To learn more about collecting soil samples and having them tested, see "Taking Soil Tests" on page 23.

A wide range of plants will thrive when soil pH is near neutral. But some, like azaleas, prefer more acid conditions.

Taking a Look at Soil Color

One simple way to learn more about your soil is to look closely at its color. If you've always lived in one place, you may think that all soil is roughly the same color. When you look closely, though, you'll see that even soils within a few feet of each other can look different, due to variations in the drainage or the organic matter content. If you travel across the country, you may see soil that is brown, black, red, yellowish, tan, white, or gray, depending on the climate and the parent material that formed the soil.

Color Cues for Humus

If you ever pass through rural Illinois or Iowa during planting season, you'll see acre after acre of dark black soil. These prairie soils, formed by hundreds or thousands of years of decaying grasses, are rich in organic matter. More specifically, they're rich in humus, which is what's left after microorganisms digest the more palatable portions of dead plants. It's humus that gives these soils their rich, dark color. Dark brown soils also tend to have a good supply of organic matter.

You can also see the effect of humus on soil color as you dig a hole in your garden. Since topsoil tends to be higher in humus than the subsoil, you'll probably notice that the top layer is darker than the underlying soil. If you don't see a darker layer on the top, that may mean you have no topsoil. (In that case, you'll need to work in lots of organic matter to get your soil in shape for a garden.)

Hues Hint at Soil Drainage

Color also can tell you how well drained your soil is, especially if you dig a hole and look at the subsoil. Red or yellow hues generally indicate well-

Dig below the surface to see your soil's true colors.

If your soil has a blue or grayish tinge, it may be a good site for plants like marsh marigolds (*Caltha palustris*) that need wet conditions.

drained soil. Soils tinged with gray or blue often form when oxygen is limited, as it is in poorly drained soils.

Some soils, rather than having a consistent coloring to the subsoil, are mottled or streaked. Areas of yellow or red may alternate with gray or blue. In these soils, drainage is erratic. Plants growing there may perform well when the roots are in well-drained parts of the soil, then suffer when the roots try to expand into soggy, poorly aerated sections.

Other Color Cues

In some western regions, the soils are high in magnesium and calcium salts that form a white crust on the surface. If the soil is high in sodium salts, it disintegrates the humus in the soil, which rises to the surface and makes the soil look black. In the East, cool, humid areas often produce soils with a thin black surface layer over a white, highly leached zone; these soils tend to be acid and low in nutrients.

You might expect darker soils to warm up faster in spring, since they would absorb more heat. But this is not the case when the dark color is due to ample organic matter. The organic matter holds lots of water, and water warms more slowly than air. As a result, light-colored mineral soils are often ready for planting a week or two sooner than dark, humus-rich sites.

A white color may indicate a sandy, highly leached layer.

A grayish cast to the soil may indicate poor drainage.

In temperate areas, soils are often a medium brown color.

Reddish soil is a common sight in hot climates.

Brush leaves and other debris off the soil where you plan to dig.

Set the soil aside as you dig a hole about 6 inches (15 cm) deep.

Take a sample from the side of the hole and let it dry; remove any debris.

Taking Soil Tests

To get the most accurate information about your soil's chemical properties, it's worth taking a little time to collect good samples and have them tested by a professional soil laboratory.

You can usually buy a soil test kit at your local Cooperative Extension Service office for a reasonable fee. The kit will contain a sample bag, data sheet, and instructions on collecting a sample and sending it to the soil-testing laboratory at your state's agricultural college. Private labs are also available and might be better prepared to give recommendations for organic fertilizers, although they are often more expensive. Your local garden center may be able to sell you the Extension Service kits or recommend a reliable soil-testing lab in your area.

Collecting Soil Samples
You can collect a soil sample anytime, although either before planting or after harvest is preferable. If you repeat the test in the future, try to collect samples at the same time of year. The soil should be just moist enough to form a loose ball when you press it in your fist, then crumble when you open your hand and poke the soil ball.

You'll need a clean spade or trowel for digging the samples, and a clean, dry plastic bucket for mixing them. If you plan to regularly collect samples in a large area, it will make your work easier if you invest in a soil auger or probe. (An auger is like a corkscrew that twists a sample from the ground; a probe is a cylinder that pulls out a neat soil core.) Also gather a sealable plastic bag and a small box for shipping the samples, or use the soil sample bag that the Cooperative Extension Service or the soil lab provides.

Get a different test done for each area of your landscape: the vegetable garden, the lawn, and the flower beds. If you have any spot where the soil is noticeably different—for example, someplace nothing grows or that's often soggy—take a separate sample from there. To collect and prepare a sample:

1. Scrape away leaves and other plant debris from the surface.
2. Use the spade or trowel to dig a hole about 6 inches (15 cm) deep (4 inches [10 cm] for lawns). Set the soil aside.
3. Shave a 1-inch (2.5 cm) thick slice from the edge of the hole and dump it in the bucket. Replace the soil you removed from the hole.
4. Repeat steps 1 through 3, collecting about five samples per 100 square feet (9.3 square meters).
5. Mix the soil in the bucket, then spread it on a newspaper to air dry.
6. Scoop about a cup of air-dried soil into the collection bag, picking out stones, roots, and other debris.
7. Ship the sample to the soil lab. Include your name and address, and tell the kind of garden the soil is from (vegetable garden, flower bed, or lawn). It's worth asking for organic fertilizer recommendations to deal with any deficiencies, though your lab may not supply them. Expect your results in 6 to 8 weeks.

LIFE IN THE SOIL

Given the human aversion to things that crawl up our legs when we're outdoors or make fuzzy green spots on our stale bread, it's probably a blessing that we don't have x-ray vision. If we did, each time we looked at the soil we'd be uneasily aware of the beetles, spiders, worms, bacteria, fungi, algae, and other organisms that live there.

As it is, most of us get through our day with nary a thought about soil organisms. And you can be fairly confident that soil organisms get through their day with nary a thought about us. Fortunately, they don't go through their day without wriggling through the soil, eating dead plants and animals, and excreting the leftovers. In this chapter, you'll discover how important the living part of your soil is in making your garden a more hospitable place for plants to grow.

"The World under Your Feet" on page 26 covers the visible and invisible creatures that live in your soil, and the different ways that they directly and indirectly affect your plants. You'll learn ways to protect the beneficial soil organisms that are already present in your garden and how to encourage even more organisms for the most productive, healthy soil.

In "Soil and Plant Growth" on page 28, you'll discover how plants interact with the soil they grow in. You'll learn just what plants get from the soil and how you can make sure your soil provides everything your plants need to thrive.

"Soil Insects and Diseases" on page 30 covers some of the troublesome organisms that live in your garden soil—from cutworms and beetle grubs to club root fungi and crown gall bacteria. Plus, you'll learn about some soil-dwelling insects and pathogens that are actually helpful to your crops.

On page 32, you'll find the "Guide to Soil Life." These entries offer photographs and specific information about some of the most common organisms that may dwell in your soil. For each organism, you'll learn more about what it is, what it (or its damage) looks like, and what role it plays in the soil.

Healthy soil is home to an incredible number and variety of organisms. Some of these are harmful to your plants; others—including many types of fungi—are important for breaking down dead tissue into nutrients and organic matter.

The World under Your Feet

An amazing number of visible and invisible organisms work together to make your soil a good place for plants to grow. Unfortunately, not all soil is hospitable to healthy populations of soil organisms. And, of course, not all soil organisms are beneficial. Learning a little about the creatures that inhabit the soil will help you encourage large populations of beneficial organisms and discourage the ones that can harm your plants.

Soil Biology 101

Scientists often group soil organisms into two broad groups: macroorganisms and microorganisms. Soil organisms that you can see with your bare eyes—for example, spiders, insects, burrowing mammals, worms, plant roots—are macroorganisms. Those that you need a microscope to see are microorganisms. Microorganisms include the multitude of soil-dwelling bacteria, fungi, and protozoa, as well as some nematodes and mites.

In both groups, there are producers, consumers, and decomposers. Producers —including plants and some specialized bacteria—are the organisms that can make their own food, either by photosynthesis or from air and minerals in the soil. Consumers are all the organisms that feed on other living creatures; these include insects, animals,

Clover roots support certain beneficial soil bacteria; in return, the bacteria supply the plant with nutrients.

and some fungi and bacteria. The third group—the decomposers—are responsible for breaking down the remainders of producers and consumers. Decomposers, mostly fungi and bacteria, release mineral nutrients that are taken up by producers, completing the nutrient cycle.

From a human perspective, some soil organisms are more desirable than others. We like the ones that decompose dead things and animal waste because they return nutrients to the soil. We also like the ones that attack soil-dwelling pests. We are considerably less fond of those organisms that attack us or our plants. Fortunately, there are many things you can do to encourage the good guys and make the bad guys less troublesome.

Encouraging Soil Life

Like other creatures, soil organisms have basic needs that must be met for them to thrive. If you prepare your garden soil with their needs in mind, these organisms will repay you many times over by releasing nutrients that will encourage strong, healthy plant growth.

Supply Plenty of Food Adding organic matter with a balanced supply of carbon and nitrogen is a key part of boosting the soil community. Most soil organisms either feed on organic matter (the decomposers) or on the organisms that feed on organic matter (the consumers).

Carbon, in the form of carbohydrates, is the main food source for most microorganisms. When carbon is in plentiful supply, these organisms multiply and can quickly use up all of the available nitrogen. That's why

---

Keep 'em Warm

Soil creatures tend to be most active at temperatures between 70°F (21°C) and 100°F (38°C). They move slower and slower until the temperature drops below 50°F (10°C), at which point most go dormant. Some succumb to extreme temperatures, but enough survive to repopulate the soil when more moderate weather returns.

If the soil organisms are sluggish after a cold winter, they may be slow in releasing available nutrients to your plants. To encourage microorganisms to get moving in the spring, rake off heavy mulches, which keep the soil cool. In the vegetable garden, you can also cover the ground with black plastic to warm the soil and get the soil creatures working to release nutrients.

your plants may turn yellow and show other nitrogen deficiency symptoms if you add lots of high-carbon material—like leaves—to your soil. A steady supply of balanced organic matter will promote a healthy population of many different soil creatures.

Add Lots of Air   Most soil organisms (including plant roots) also need oxygen to survive. Oxygen is plentiful in loose, well-drained soil with good soil structure. In heavy (clayey), poorly drained, or compacted soils, oxygen is limited. If oxygen is scarce, the microorganisms may use it up before plants can get at it. Plus, the lack of oxygen favors microorganisms that often produce substances toxic to plants.

If your soil isn't too wet, digging or tilling is a fast and easy way to add lots of air. Adding organic matter also helps to loosen heavy soil and promote good soil structure. If your soil is poorly drained, you may need to build raised beds or dig drains to provide the right conditions for a healthy soil community.

Be warned that too much oxygen can be a problem as well. When you turn the soil, the large amount of oxygen that gets mixed in stimulates an organic-matter feeding frenzy among the underworld

As rocks break down, they produce mineral-rich soil that can support a wide variety of plants and animals.

Moles, voles, gophers, and other soil-dwelling creatures help to stir the soil as they burrow in search of food.

denizens. Adding organic matter any time you turn the soil keeps the supply from being depleted.

Keep the Soil Evenly Moist   When it comes to water, soil organisms like what most plants like— enough water to keep the soil moist but not soggy. Excess water in the soil fills the pore spaces that would normally contain air. Roots and many other soil organisms can suffocate without some oxygen. If your soil tends to be very wet, either choose adapted plants or build raised beds. If you have well-drained soil, work in some organic matter and use mulch to keep the soil evenly moist; irrigate as needed during dry spells.

Adding organic matter to your soil encourages beneficial soil organisms and promotes healthy plant growth.

Healthy, well-prepared garden soil will support your plants from seedling stage to flowering and fruiting.

Soil and Plant Growth

Throughout the life of your plants, the soil provides many of the things those plants need to germinate, grow, and thrive. Understanding how your plants interact with the soil will help you manage your garden to provide the best possible growing conditions.

Start with the Seed

The first two things a seed needs are warmth and water. If the soil is too cold or too dry, the seed remains dormant. This makes sense; it would do a seed little good to germinate if it's still winter or if there isn't enough water around to support growth.

Warmth is usually more reliable than water. Soil temperatures don't change as rapidly as air temperatures, so once the soil is warm enough for growth to begin—and that temperature varies, depending on the plant species—it usually stays warm enough for growth to continue. If you want to warm the soil more quickly in spring, there are a few things you can do: remove heavy mulches, cover the soil with black plastic, or plant in raised beds.

Water is less dependable than warmth. If the soil dries out after germination begins, the young seedling

Most plants prefer well-drained soil, but some, like celery, take wetter conditions.

soon dies. Soils with good structure increase the odds that the seed will germinate; the soil particles are fine enough to closely surround the seed, holding moisture against it. Clayey soils hold too much moisture, while loose, sandy soils may dry out too quickly. Improving your soil by digging and adding organic matter can help keep moisture at the ideal level for seedling growth.

Shoots and Roots

When the seed germinates, it puts out a temporary root, called the primary root or radicle. The radicle stores some of the food that provides the energy that the first aboveground shoot needs to push up through the soil (the rest is in the seed leaves, which are the leaf-like parts attached to the shoot). The radicle also anchors the plant, so the shoot won't blow or wash away.

About the time the first shoot reaches the soil surface, lateral roots begin to grow from the radicle. Like the radicle, the lateral roots anchor the plant in the soil. Throughout most of the plant's life, the roots expand to counterbalance the aboveground parts of the plant. In many cases, the root mass is larger than that of the stems and leaves.

As roots grow, they produce chemical compounds that help make nutrients more soluble and therefore more available to the plant. Throughout their life, roots absorb water and dissolved nutrients from the soil. When they die, the roots add organic matter to the soil.

The chemicals roots produce and the dead cells they shed create an environment that soil microorganisms

Seedlings thrive in warm, well-drained soil. Raised beds or black plastic mulches can help heat up cold spring soil.

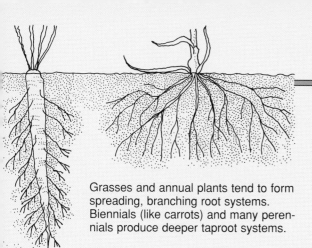

Grasses and annual plants tend to form spreading, branching root systems. Biennials (like carrots) and many perennials produce deeper taproot systems.

find attractive. They multiply more rapidly in the root zone than they do in the surrounding soil. As a result, organic matter breaks down faster, making nutrients more available in the soil the roots touch.

All the things you do to encourage soil organisms—providing air, moisture, and ample amounts of organic matter—will help ensure a steady supply of nutrients when and where plants need them. Plus, the moist, well-aerated, fertile conditions that promote a healthy soil community also provide ideal conditions for root growth. More roots encourage more organisms, which release more nutrients that promote more roots—a productive natural cycle.

Growth and Flowering

As plants grow, the water and nutrients the roots absorb flow up through the plant to the leaves and stems. During photosynthesis, the leaves and stems convert the water and nutrients to sugars; the sugars then flow down to the roots to be stored as carbohydrates—food energy.

Annual roots don't grow very deep, but they do spread wide to get the nutrients the plants need for fast growth.

Roots Need to Breathe, Too

For healthy growth, plant roots need plenty of oxygen. Roots breathe—respire—just as people do, taking in oxygen and releasing carbon dioxide. While the leaves and stems can absorb oxygen from above ground, the roots must draw it from the spaces between the various soil particles.

In the root zone, ideally about half of those spaces hold air; that percentage decreases deeper in the soil. The actual amount of air in your soil varies, depending on how well the soil drains and how loose the soil structure is. In poorly drained soils, roots grow more slowly because they get less oxygen. If the ground is compacted, or if the root zone is covered with a layer of fill or concrete, roots will also be deprived of oxygen.

So how can you make sure your soil has enough air? Adding ample amounts of organic matter can help loosen heavy soils; building raised beds will add enough well-aerated rooting room for many plants. Avoid adding thick layers of soil or heavy mulches that can keep the soil wet and cause roots to suffocate.

Before it flowers and sets seed, the plant uses that energy for growth. While the stems and leaves are growing, the roots rapidly expand both out and down through the soil to reach water and nutrients. Once the plant flowers and the seed ripens, root growth slows as more energy is channeled to these demanding processes.

If the plant is an annual, it grows old and dies after the seed ripens. Its decaying roots, leaves, and stems return nutrients to the soil. If the plant is a perennial, it stores carbohydrates in its roots to use to start growing in the spring. Its leaves and stems die back and decay, adding nutrients to the soil to start the cycle over.

Deep digging is critical for success with long-rooted crops like parsnips and carrots.

Soil Insects and Diseases

Bad organisms, like bad people, make the news most often. Most gardeners know more about soil-dwelling insects and diseases that assault plants than ones that make plants' lives easier. Perhaps that's because the do-gooders go about their business so constantly that we don't notice their efforts. We do notice, however, when a pest topples our transplants in the night. Both the beneficial and harmful critters are a natural part of garden soil. The trick is to encourage the good guys and discourage the troublemakers.

Insects under the Ground

Many soil-dwelling insects that attack plants are the immature, larval stage of moths and beetles. These wormy insects hatch from eggs, then grow and feed in

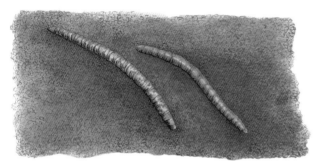

the soil until they're ready to pupate, become adults, and fly off. The larvae of flies are called maggots, while those of beetles are called grubs, and those of moths and butterflies are called caterpillars.

Among the most damaging larvae are cutworms, various grubs, and a few tunneling maggots. Cutworms are caterpillars that curl around the base of young stems, chewing through them until the plant falls over. Grubs are more fond of roots, especially the

Soilborne problems—like nematode damage—can be difficult to diagnose, since the cause is rarely easy to see.

roots of grasses. Maggots tunnel their way into roots and bulbs, making the damaged plant tissue prone to rot-causing bacteria. Slugs and some caterpillars will crawl up plants to chew holes in leaves.

Fortunately for us, insect pests have enemies that attack them. Ground beetles, for example, are aggressive enough to eat just about anything that crawls through the soil. Moles eat grubs and other insects (although their tunnels may also leave ridges in the lawn). Hundreds of parasites, such as mites and nematodes, attack soil insects, feeding on them both from outside and inside their bodies.

Besides eating plant pests, many soil-dwelling insects help plants in other ways, too. They loosen the soil as they crawl through it, improving aeration and drainage and making channels that roots can grow into. They chew and tear dead plant tissue, making the tissue easier for soil microorganisms to digest. And when they die, the nutrients in their decomposing bodies become available to plants.

The same things that you do to encourage beneficial soil organisms—adding organic matter, improving drainage, and supplying adequate moisture—will promote healthy populations of beneficial soil insects. Some of the larger beneficials, like ground beetles and rove beetles, appreciate extra shelter. Plant cover crops and provide mulches like newspaper

Crown gall is a bacterial disease that causes knobby growths on the stems of roses, forsythias, and euonymus.

During the day, slugs hide in cool and dark spots under leaves and mulches; at night, they come out to feed on plants.

or compost; permanent beds and stepping-stone paths will also provide useful hiding places.

Just as you can buy beneficial insects like lacewings to control aboveground pests, you can also purchase some organisms to control soil-dwelling pests. Some garden catalogs sell beneficial nematodes that can control many kinds of pests, including onion maggots, black vine weevils, cutworms, and wireworms. Dust milky disease spores on your lawn to help control Japanese beetle grubs and several related beetles.

Make Way for Microorganisms

Even though you can't see them working, microscopic bacteria, fungi, and actinomycetes are responsible for the bulk of the activity that takes place in the soil.

Fungi, bacteria, and actinomycetes all decompose organic matter, returning the nutrients to the soil. Fungi also improve soil structure by producing thread-like structures that help bind the soil particles together. Beneficial nitrogen-fixing bacteria work with plants like peas and beans to take nitrogen gas from the atmosphere and convert it to a form of nitrogen that plants can use.

These three groups of microorganisms also include species that cause diseases. Verticillium and Fusarium wilts, damping-off, club root, and crown gall are some of the best-known and most troublesome soilborne diseases. They can infest roots, bulbs, tubers, and crowns—especially those damaged by insects or garden tools. These microorganisms can reach leaves and stems in splashing water and travel between plants on a film of water.

Disease-causing soil microorganisms vary in their ability to adapt to different host plants. Some only infect a certain plant, and if that plant isn't grown for a year or two, the microorganisms die out. Others are less picky, readily attacking many plants.

You can control some diseases by changing the soil environment. Lowering the pH can control potato scab, which is caused by an actinomycete. Raising it to about 7.2 helps control club root, a fungal disease that affects plants in the cabbage family. Usually, though, it's not practical to drastically change your soil's pH just for disease control; you could be doing more harm than good by upsetting the natural balance of soil organisms.

Crop rotation—planting crops in different areas of the garden each year—can help starve out some disease-causing organisms; allow at least a year or two—and preferably more—before planting a particular crop in the same place. Compost contains a host of beneficial, disease-suppressing microorganisms that can help keep pathogens under control—just one more reason to add generous quantities of compost to your soil.

Some fungi feed on living plants; others help to break down plant material that has already died.

ROOTS

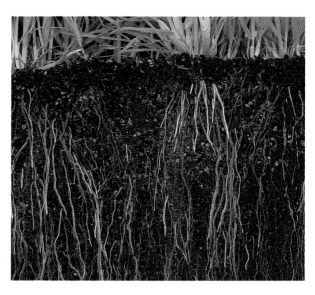

Living roots release organic materials that are a source of food for microorganisms; dead roots add organic matter to the soil. Roots also help hold the soil, preventing erosion.

WHAT THEY ARE: The belowground portion of plants that absorbs water and dissolved nutrients.

WHAT THEY LOOK LIKE: Depending on the plant, roots range from a few inches to several feet long. Some root systems, like those of grasses, are made up of many branched roots that are all roughly the same length and diameter; these are known as fibrous roots. In other cases, the first root that develops from a seedling increases in length and width, and shorter, thinner roots form along the sides; this is known as a taproot system. (Taproots are fairly common among biennials, like carrots, and perennials, such as dandelions.) Just above the tip of each root are thousands of thin, fine root hairs that cling tightly to soil particles.

WHAT THEY DO: Roots perform many important functions. Besides anchoring plants in the soil, they also absorb the water and nutrients needed for plant growth. Roots can also help break up hard, tight soil as they grow and expand.

HOW TO ENCOURAGE: Roots generally thrive in soil that is loose and has an even supply of moisture. Add organic matter to break up heavy, clayey soil or to increase the moisture-holding capacity of dry, sandy soil. Organic mulches can also help to keep the soil moist and at a fairly even temperature, encouraging good root growth.

MOLES

Moles are often mistakenly blamed for eating roots and bulbs. The actual culprits are usually mice or voles, which use the mole tunnels to reach your garden.

WHAT THEY ARE: Subterranean insect-eating mammals.

WHAT THEY LOOK LIKE: Moles are plump, dark, furry animals with pointed, hairless noses. Their eyes may be very tiny or covered by skin. Moles are about 5–8 inches (12.5–20 cm) long.

WHAT THEY DO: Moles dig miles of tunnels in their constant search for food. They usually eat insects (especially beetle grubs) and earthworms, but they will occasionally feed on plant roots. The tunnels they live and feed in during mild weather are near the surface, often bordering fences, buildings, and other protected areas. Moles dig a deeper tunnel system to live and nest in when the weather is cold.

Many gardeners dislike moles because their tunnels can create ridges beneath the lawn that mar its appearance. Also, the roots of plants growing above a tunnel can grow into the air-filled space and dry out, causing stripes of drying grass. In general, though, moles are beneficial. They eat many pest insects, and their digging churns and aerates the soil.

HOW TO DISCOURAGE: Applying spores of milky disease (a bacterial disease that affects many kinds of grubs) may help reduce pest populations and discourage moles. Strong vibrations can also bother moles, so whirligigs, wind jugs, and other noise-making devices set on or into the soil can sometimes chase them off.

EARTHWORMS

A large population of earthworms is a good indication of healthy soil. You can encourage earthworms by adding organic matter such as a mulch or a soil amendment.

WHAT THEY ARE: Soft-bodied, segmented scavengers.

WHAT THEY LOOK LIKE: Earthworms range in color from brown to reddish brown to pink. Their segmented bodies are usually 4–6 inches (10–15 cm) long.

WHAT THEY DO: As they tunnel and feed, earthworms improve soil structure and fertility, making it more productive. They eat soil for the organic matter it contains, grinding it and absorbing some of the dissolved minerals as the material passes through their bodies. Earthworms can consume their own weight in soil each day.

Their excretions, which are called castings, are high in organic matter, beneficial bacteria, nitrogen, phosphorus, potassium, and micronutrients; they have a nearly neutral pH. A healthy worm population can digest a 1-inch (2.5 cm) layer of organic matter in a few months and leave behind 5½ ounces (150 g) per worm of nutrient-rich castings. The castings help to improve soil structure by increasing the size and stability of soil particles.

Earthworms are also beneficial by helping to mix the soil, carrying organic matter deep into the soil, and bringing subsoil to the surface. A healthy worm population can bring 4–8 pounds (1.8–3.6 kg) of subsoil to the surface per 100-square-foot (9.3 sq m) area. Their burrows, which can be up to 6 feet (1.8 m) deep, improve aeration and drainage.

Small mounds of castings on the soil surface are a sign of earthworm activity. Collect the castings for use as a fertilizer in the garden, or rake them out over the lawn.

Cutworms live near the soil surface and feed on young plant stems at night. Damage is easier to prevent than control; protect seedling stems with paper or plastic collars.

The burrows also create channels that growing roots can use.

Earthworms thrive in moist, well-aerated soil with lots of organic matter. They are more numerous in loamy soil than in dry, sandy soil or oxygen-deficient, clayey soil. Some tolerate a low pH, but most prefer a pH near neutral. Different species are adapted to different temperatures. *Lumbricus terrestris.* the species common in gardens, is most active when the soil temperature is around 50°F (10°C); that's why maximum worm activity takes place in fall and spring. During hot or cold weather, earthworms move deeper into the soil. Red worms (*Lumbricus rubellus*) or brandling worms (*Eisenia foetida*), which are often sold as fish bait, tolerate heat well enough to live in a compost pile.

HOW TO ENCOURAGE: You can encourage healthy populations of earthworms by adding plenty of organic matter to the soil. Avoid the use of pesticides and synthetic fertilizers, which can dissolve to form concentrated salt solutions that are caustic to earthworms. You can also buy earthworms to add to your garden, although a year or two of working in and mulching with organic matter should boost existing worm populations dramatically.

WHAT THEY ARE: The larval stage of any one of hundreds of small brown or gray moths.

WHAT THEY LOOK LIKE: These plump, greasy-looking caterpillars are about 1–2 inches (2.5–5 cm) long. They can be gray, brown, red, or greenish white and may have stripes or patches. They have shiny heads and may coil into a ball when touched.

WHAT THEY DO: Cutworms feed at night, curling around the stems of young plants and sometimes severing them at or just below the soil level. Some species overwinter as eggs and hatch during the first warm days of spring to attack early seedlings. Other species don't emerge until late May. The larvae feed for a month or two, then pupate and turn into adults by the end of the summer. They are more of a problem in plots that were covered with weeds or sod the previous year.

HOW TO DISCOURAGE: If cutworms are a problem in your garden, dig around the base of damaged transplants in the morning and destroy larvae that are hiding below the soil surface. Beneficial nematodes may also help control these pests. You can prevent their damage by surrounding your transplants with paper, cardboard, or plastic collars pushed halfway into the soil. (The collars will prevent the cutworm from wrapping around the stem.)

GRUBS

Grubs attract hungry birds, so busy flocks are one clue to a grub infestation. Grubs also attract moles, skunks, and other insect-eating mammals to your lawn or garden.

WHAT THEY ARE: The immature, or larval, stage in the life cycle of beetles, including Japanese beetles, May or June beetles, and weevils.

WHAT THEY LOOK LIKE: Grubs are usually fat, whitish, and curled into a C-shape. They vary from 1/2–1 inch (12–25 mm) long. Adults vary in appearance, depending on the species.

WHAT THEY DO: Grubs usually eat the same kind of food as their adult stage. Many kinds of grubs feed on the roots of plants, especially sod. If the infestation is heavy—about 10 larvae per square foot (9 sq cm)—the grubs can sever so many roots that it's possible to roll up the sod like a carpet. They can also be a problem in new vegetable, flower, and shrub beds for the first few years after the sod is removed.

HOW TO DISCOURAGE: Beneficial nematodes and bacterial diseases like milky disease can keep grub populations in check.

HOW TO ENCOURAGE: Although most gardeners think of all grubs as pests, this isn't really the case. The larvae of ground beetles and tiger beetles, for instance, attack many kinds of soil-dwelling insects; the larvae of blister beetles prey on grasshopper eggs. Permanent plantings, like perennial beds, cover crops, and shrub borders, provide shelter for these beneficial beetle grubs.

GROUND BEETLES

Ground beetles are important predators of some of the most destructive garden pests, including slugs, snails, and caterpillars, both above and below the soil surface.

WHAT THEY ARE: Ground beetles make up one of the largest families of beetles, with over 2,500 species.

WHAT THEY LOOK LIKE: Adults can be black, brown, blue, or green. They have long legs and a shiny oval body ranging from 3/4–1 inch (18–25 mm) long. The larvae are dark, with ten body segments that taper toward the rear.

WHAT THEY DO: Adults and larvae feed voraciously on other soil dwellers, both harmful and beneficial. They are particularly valued by gardeners because they prey on slugs, caterpillars, and cutworms. Adult ground beetles may even pursue prey that lives aboveground, like Colorado potato beetle larvae and gypsy moth caterpillars.

HOW TO ENCOURAGE: During the day, many species of ground beetles hide under fallen leaves, mulches, rocks, and other cover—the same conditions that attract much of their prey. Permanent beds and perennial plantings, such as groundcovers and cover crops, also provide shelter for the beetles.

MILLIPEDES

Millipedes may feed on plant roots if other food is scarce, but they mostly help to decompose decaying organic materials in the soil and the compost pile.

WHAT THEY ARE: Many-legged invertebrate animals.

WHAT THEY LOOK LIKE: Millipedes resemble short, slender worms or caterpillars. Their cylindrical bodies, which range from $^1/_2$–$1^1/_2$ inches (12–37 mm) long, are divided into many segments, each with two pairs of legs. Millipedes move slowly and may curl up when touched.

WHAT THEY DO: Millipedes often live in compost piles, where they feed on decaying organic matter. When their populations are high, they may resort to eating plant roots, seeds, and germinating seedlings. When they do, they will eat almost any plant, but they seldom do enough damage to warrant alarm.

    Millipedes are sometimes confused with centipedes, carnivorous creatures that prey on other soil dwellers including insects and insect larvae. Centipedes are faster moving than millipedes and have a flattened, not rounded, body with one pair of legs per segment. Like millipedes, centipedes are usually considered to be beneficial, though they occasionally may feed on plants and earthworms.

HOW TO DISCOURAGE: Control is seldom needed. If millipede populations are high, try sprinkling diatomaceous earth (a powder available from many garden centers or garden-supply catalogs) near rows of germinating seeds.

WIREWORMS

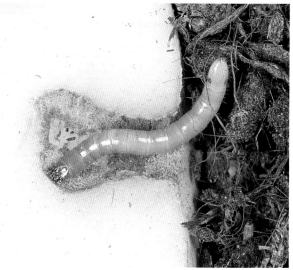

To reduce wireworm populations, trap them in pieces of potato impaled on sticks and buried in the soil in spring; after a few days, remove and destroy infested pieces.

WHAT THEY ARE: The larval stage of click beetles. (The adults are so named because they make a clicking sound as they flip from their backs to their feet.)

WHAT THEY LOOK LIKE: Wireworms resemble small, thin worms, except that their skin is hard and jointed. They are yellow to reddish brown and up to $1^1/_2$ inches (3.7 cm) long, with three sets of legs just behind the head. The adults are $^1/_3$–$^3/_4$-inch (8–20 mm) long, dull, brownish beetles with wide grooves or stripes on their wings.

WHAT THEY DO: The larvae bore into seeds, roots, tubers, and bulbs to feed. They also eat seedlings, especially of vegetables. They can stunt or kill plants. They are particularly a problem in new gardens for about 2 years after the sod is removed. (Once that plentiful and steady food source is gone, the wireworms voraciously attack whatever is planted where the grass once grew.) Eventually their populations die back to keep in balance with the food supply.

HOW TO DISCOURAGE: Beneficial nematodes may help keep wireworms under control. Another control method is cultivating the soil weekly for 4–6 weeks in fall, which will expose the larvae to birds and other predators.

Maggots

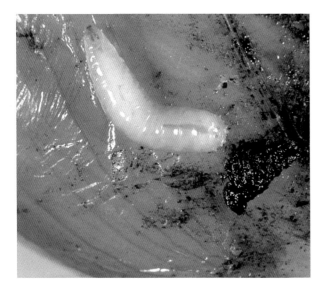

Rotating planting sites and shielding plants with floating row covers are two effective ways to help protect your cabbage-family and onion crops from maggot damage.

WHAT THEY ARE: The larval stage of flies.

WHAT THEY LOOK LIKE: Cabbage maggots are white with tapered bodies; the adults are long-legged gray flies. Onion maggots are white with blunt bodies; the adults are gray, bristly, and humpbacked. The maggots and adults for both are about $^1/_4$ inch (6 mm) long.

WHAT THEY DO: Cabbage maggots attack the roots of plants in the cabbage family, including cabbage, kale, broccoli, and cauliflower. They also infest some root crops, such as radishes and turnips. They bore into the root, stunting the plant. The first sign of an infestation is the plant wilting at midday. Cabbage maggot damage also provides an easy entrance for disease organisms. These pests are especially troublesome in Northern gardens.

Onion maggots burrow into developing onions, shallots, and leeks. They kill young plants and hollow out the bulbs of older ones, stunting and providing entry points for disease organisms. Onion maggots are primarily a problem in the northern half of the United States as well as Canada.

HOW TO DISCOURAGE: Plant cabbage-family and onion crops in different spots each year and protect them with floating row covers. Remove and destroy the roots of susceptible plants when harvesting the tops; cultivate the soil in fall to expose the pupal stage to damaging winter cold.

Nematodes

Pest nematodes feed on the roots, stems, and leaves of many plants. They cause excessive root branching, damaged and distorted roots, or leaves with knots and galls.

WHAT THEY ARE: Small worm-like animals that live in soil or water and feed on plants or other animals as predators or parasites. They may be harmful (such as those that feed on plants) or beneficial (like those that are parasitic on weevils, borers, and other garden pests).

WHAT THEY LOOK LIKE: Nematodes resemble translucent worms with unsegmented bodies. The beneficial species can be from $^1/_{25}$ inch to several inches (1–75 mm) long. Most plant-damaging species are microscopic, ranging from $^1/_{125}$–$^1/_{25}$ inch (0.2–1 mm) long.

WHAT THEY DO: Nematodes feed by poking their sharp mouthparts into their victim's cells, injecting saliva to soften things up, and sucking out the contents. They may feed from the outside or crawl into the victim to be an internal parasite. Beneficial nematodes attack a wide variety of pests, including borers, root weevils, and rootworms. As they feed, they release a bacterium that paralyzes and kills the host.

HOW TO DISCOURAGE: Crop rotation and solarization can control pest nematodes; see "Controlling Disease Problems" on page 114 for details.

HOW TO ENCOURAGE: You can buy several kinds of insect-parasitic nematodes from garden-supply catalogs to add to your soil to control garden pests.

FUNGI

Thousands of species of fungi have been identified, including molds, yeasts, and mushrooms. Many kinds of fungi are beneficial in the garden; others cause plant diseases.

Fungi are the most adaptable soil microorganism, although their numbers fluctuate with soil conditions. They are able to reproduce in soil that is too acid for most bacteria.

WHAT THEY ARE: Fungi are a diverse group of organisms that get their nutrients from live or decomposing organic material.

WHAT THEY LOOK LIKE: Some fungi are microscopic; others—like the bracket or shelf fungus that forms on decaying wood—can be as big as your hand. Most fungi form multicelled bodies called mycelium, made up microscopic filaments. These strands are called hyphae and can extend for long distances through the soil. Many fungi also form fruiting bodies that release spores. Mushrooms are one obvious type of fruiting body. Plant-attacking fungi may have a fuzzy or powdery appearance on leaves, stems, or other plant parts.

WHAT THEY DO: Many gardeners think of all fungi as harmful. It's true that soil-dwelling parasitic fungi are responsible for most of the soilborne plant diseases. Among the most notable are those that cause wilt diseases—such as oak wilt, Verticillium wilt, and Fusarium wilt—which clog stems, blocking the flow of water and nutrients and causing the plant to die. Fungi also cause damping-off, a disease that kills off young seedlings before or shortly after they emerge. Other common fungal diseases include root rot and club root.

Not all fungi are troublesome, though. Many are saprophytic, which means they draw energy from dead plants and animals. These fungi play a vital role in the decomposition process. Other fungi are parasites—they feed on insects and other soil-dwelling organisms.

They play a greater role in decomposition than bacteria because they digest a wider range of materials. Fungi also improve soil structure and stability because the mats of mycelium bind soil particles.

One special group of fungi extends its mycelium into the roots of plants. The combination of the root and fungus is called mycorrhiza. The relationship benefits both the fungus and the plant: The plant's roots provide carbohydrates for the fungus, while the fungus helps the plant to better absorb nutrients (especially phosphorus) and water. Natural mycorrhizal associations are widespread and occur on vegetables, ornamentals, trees, and other types of plants.

HOW TO DISCOURAGE: Soil solarization will kill some fungi; see "Solarize the Soil" on page 115 for details. In many cases, using resistant plants can help minimize problems. Crop rotation may help in some cases, although many parasitic fungi can live in the soil for several years without their preferred host plants.

HOW TO ENCOURAGE: Working ample amounts of compost into your garden is a good way to provide ideal conditions for beneficial soil fungi.

BACTERIA AND ACTINOMYCETES

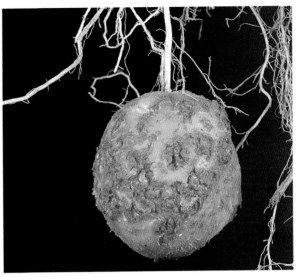

Some beneficial bacteria live in round galls on the roots of legumes, like peas and beans. These bacteria convert nitrogen from the air into a form that plants can use.

Many actinomycetes are important decomposers; they work on tough substances that bacteria and fungi leave behind. Other actinomycetes cause diseases like potato scab.

WHAT THEY ARE: Bacteria are microscopic, single-celled organisms. Actinomycetes are a particular type of bacteria that forms branching filaments, similar to a fungus.

WHAT THEY LOOK LIKE: Bacteria may be round, spiral, straight, or thread-like. Most soil-dwelling bacteria are straight or rod-shaped. Actinomycetes are branched and thread-like.

WHAT THEY DO: Some of the most important beneficial bacteria are those that can "fix" nitrogen. These bacteria absorb nitrogen gas from the air and convert it into a form their bodies can use. When these bacteria decompose, the "fixed" nitrogen enters the food chain, becoming available first to plants and soil organisms, then to larger animals.

Some nitrogen-fixing bacteria are free-living; they aren't associated with any plant or insect. Other nitrogen-fixers live in a symbiotic relationship with plants. In a symbiotic association, both organisms benefit from the relationship: The bacteria get energy from carbohydrates in the roots, and the host plant gets nitrogen. The best-known genus of nitrogen-fixing bacteria is *Rhizobium*. These bacteria live inside tiny nodules on the roots of legumes such as alfalfa, clover, peas, beans, and honey locust trees. Legumes are often grown in crop rotations as green manures or cover crops to add nitrogen to the soil.

Some types of actinomycetes are also involved with nitrogen fixation on non-legume plants like alders (*Alnus* spp.) and bayberries (*Myrica* spp.). Many also produce antibiotics (like streptomycin) that inhibit the activity of other microorganisms.

While the majority of bacteria play a vital role in soil health, there are some kinds that are harmful. About 200 species of bacteria cause diseases such as wilts, galls, cankers, leaf spots, and soft rots. A few types of actinomycetes may cause plant diseases, including potato scab.

HOW TO DISCOURAGE: Disease-causing bacteria are very difficult to control, and infected plants must be destroyed. Using resistant cultivars is one of the best ways to deal with troublesome bacterial diseases. Actinomycetes are particularly sensitive to acid soil, so you can often prevent potato scab damage by adjusting the soil pH to 5.0 or less.

HOW TO ENCOURAGE: Maintaining healthy soil that provides good conditions for plant growth can also help to ensure a favorable balance of beneficial bacteria. You can also buy some nitrogen-fixing bacteria in a powder form, called an inoculant. This powder, available from many garden centers and seed suppliers, is applied to seeds of legumes to ensure that the right bacteria are present in the soil. Different species of bacteria work with different plants, so be sure to buy the right kind for your crop.

BUILDING SOIL ORGANIC MATTER

Organic matter is the decayed remains of once-living plants, animals, and soil organisms. That's not exactly glamorous, but the way organic matter improves soils is so phenomenal that it's easy to overlook its lowly beginnings.

In "Understanding Soil Structure" on page 18, you learned how important organic matter is in developing a loose, easy-to-dig soil. But that's not all: Organic matter has other phenomenal qualities as well. For example, a layer of partially decomposed organic matter on the soil surface has enough bulk to smother weeds and keep moisture from evaporating from the soil. Organic matter also is a food for soil microorganisms. Once it decays thoroughly and becomes mixed with the soil, organic matter works like a sponge, absorbing nearly its own weight in water without becoming soggy—that's particularly helpful for sandy soils or those in dry regions. Decayed organic matter also loosens up clays, making them less sticky and improving soil structure. And it holds nutrients on its surfaces, releasing them slowly into the soil water for plants to absorb. In fact, decayed organic matter accounts for half of the soil's ability to hold and release nutrients.

In this chapter, you'll learn how to manage organic matter in a way best suited to your soil's needs. "Understanding Soil Organic Matter" on page 42 discusses all the great things that organic matter can do to help make your soil healthy and productive. In "Creating Great Compost" on page 44, you'll discover how to recycle kitchen scraps, garden trimmings, and other plant debris into a free source of rich organic matter.

"Making the Most of Mulch" on page 48 explains the many benefits of using organic mulches in the garden and offers tips for choosing and using the right mulch for your needs. See "Organic Mulches," starting on page 52, for specific information on 15 common organic mulch materials, including benefits, drawbacks, sources, and application tips.

Besides composting and mulching, you can also protect and improve your soil by raising special crops. "Growing Cover Crops and Green Manures" on page 60 covers the basics of planting and managing these soil-enriching crops. To find out more about specific crops you can grow, including best climate and site, soil and moisture needs, and growing guidelines, see "Cover Crops and Green Manures," starting on page 62.

Healthy soil builds healthy plants. Your role in the cycle is keeping the soil stocked with organic matter to provide ideal conditions for beneficial soil organisms and good root growth.

Understanding Soil Organic Matter

If you poke around in the very top soil layer in woods or a meadow, you can identify organic matter in a nearly original state. Most plentiful are decaying plant parts such as roots, stems, leaves, flowers, and fruit. The deeper you dig, the less identifiable the litter becomes. That's because organisms, both visible and microscopic, have been digesting the organic residues into a more stable end product, called humus.

Many gardeners use the terms "organic matter" and "humus" interchangeably, but these really do not mean the same thing. It's easier to think of them as two ends of a continuum, with raw organic matter (like dead leaves and grass clippings) at one end and decay-resistant humus at the other.

Humus is dark brown or black and crumbly, with an earthy smell. It mostly consists of plant components that resist decay, such as wax and lignin, mixed with substances created by

Don't throw away extra grass clippings—use them as a mulch or work them into the soil to add organic matter.

microorganisms. In early stages of its formation, humus still has enough digestible components to be food for microorganisms, which release the nutrients to your plants. Once the easily eaten portions are gone, humus can last in the soil for centuries. It is this stable form of humus that improves your soil's structure and its ability to keep water and nutrients from draining away.

Keeping the Cycle Going

Increasing the organic matter (and, in turn, the humus level) of your soil isn't quite as simple as dumping on a layer of leaves or grass clippings every few years. But it's not a difficult matter either. The trick is remembering that organic matter and soil microorganisms are linked in a cycle. You can manage organic matter to encourage microorganisms, which in turn decides how effective it is to add organic matter. The goal is to keep a balance: Too much microorganism activity and the organic matter supply is depleted; too little activity and too much organic matter accumulates.

Soil microorganisms and plants thrive with water, warmth, oxygen, a moderate pH, and a balanced supply of nutrients from organic matter. When conditions are

ideal for the microorganisms, adding a regular supply of organic matter can keep the population at optimum levels; in return, your plants will benefit from the good growing conditions and ample supply of available nutrients.

Some gardening conditions make it a real challenge to keep soil organic matter at the right level. For example, organic matter breaks down faster when there's plenty of oxygen. So it might decay too rapidly in sandy soils, or those that are hoed or turned often, because oxygen is too plentiful. On the other hand, the

Organic matter acts like a sponge in the soil, absorbing extra water and releasing the moisture when your plants need it.

As these leaves break down, they'll return nutrients to the soil; roots will take in the nutrients for next year's growth.

breakdown of organic matter may proceed too slowly to meet your plants' needs in soggy or compacted clay soils, where there's little oxygen.

Building Healthy Soil

How will you know if your soil has the right level of organic matter? Dig around in the top layer and take a look at the soil. If you can see some partially recognizable material—a few crumbled leaves, some clumpy roots—your soil is probably in good shape. If you can't see any organic material at all, it's definitely time for you to add some.

If you see lots of raw material—old broccoli stems that you turned in last fall, whole leaves, undecomposed root clumps—your soil needs some help. If the soil isn't too wet, digging or tilling may add some needed oxygen. In wet soil, you may need to build raised beds to improve drainage. If the debris is high in carbon—like old leaves and stems—try adding some nitrogen, in the form of fresh grass clippings or kitchen scraps. This may help get those sluggish microorganisms back in action.

Both sandy soils and clayey soils will eventually become less troublesome if you add lots of organic matter. Work in a 2- to 3-inch (5 to 7.5 cm) layer of compost before planting, and keep a 1- to 3-inch (2.5 to 7.5 cm) layer of organic mulch on the soil during the growing season. In the vegetable garden, a green manure crop is an excellent source of organic matter.

How often you'll need to reapply organic matter also depends on where you live. In general, organic matter is short-lived in the warm, moist soils of the southeastern United States; it can break down so fast that its nutrients wash from the soil before plants use them. Warm-climate gardeners may want to make smaller but more frequent applications. Organic matter tends to be slowly available in excessively acid or alkaline soils or in cool regions. If you have any of these conditions, one or two applications a year may be enough to keep the right balance of organic matter.

Super Sources of Organic Matter

Whether you have a soil that burns organic matter quickly or slowly, it's likely that your garden will benefit from added organic matter. More and more gardeners are discovering the benefits of making and using compost; you'll learn how to make your own in "Creating Great Compost" on page 44. Mulching with organic matter is another way to keep soil and plants in good condition; see "Making the Most of Mulch" on page 48 for details. If you have garden beds that are empty for at least part of the year—like in the vegetable garden—cover crops and green manures are easy and effective ways to add lots of fresh organic matter; "Cover Crops and Green Manures," starting on page 62, will give you the basics.

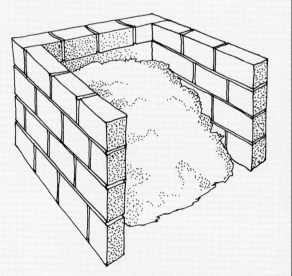

Homemade compost is a cheap source of organic matter for your garden; you'll use all you can make!

Compost is a key part of a healthy organic garden. You can work it into the soil, use it as a mulch, and even brew it into a tea to give your plants a liquid nutrient boost.

Creating Great Compost

Whether your garden is large or small, whether you grow vegetables or flowers, you can enjoy the benefits of making and using compost. This "black gold" is a free source of balanced nutrients and organic matter that you can use as a fertilizer, mulch, or soil conditioner. Making compost is also a great way to recycle garden wastes—like leaves, stems, and clippings—that don't belong in landfills; you can even add vegetable peelings, houseplant trimmings, and other organic material that may otherwise end up being wasted in your household trash. For all of these reasons, composting is the right thing to do.

Composting Myths and Realities

At this point, you may wonder why everyone doesn't make compost. Perhaps it's because they've gotten the idea that it's too complicated or that it takes up too much room, that it looks messy, or that it smells.

Fortunately, properly made compost doesn't have to be any of these things.

Although some gardeners have raised composting to an art form, basic composting requires little physical effort and even less thought. After all, the phenomenon that makes composting possible —decomposition of organic matter by soil microorganisms—was going on long before the first human wondered what to do with all those grass clippings.

At the heart of the composting process is the compost pile. If you have the room and don't mind the look, the pile can be pretty informal—just a heap where you toss plant debris and forget about it. If you have limited space or if you like things to look tidy and organized, you can buy or make a simple or elaborate structure to contain the material (see "Enclosing Your Compost" for details). If space is really at a premium, look into an indoor worm composting system, available from many garden-supply catalogs.

If you build your compost pile with the right balance of ingredients, it won't have an offensive odor. If you do notice a smell, see "Compost Troubleshooting" on page 46 to find out what the problem is and how to fix it.

If you have room, build several piles so you'll always have one ready to use.

Compost needs moisture to break down. You may have to water the pile.

A tarp can help hold in moisture and keep rain from washing out nutrients.

Enclosing Your Compost

While you can compost quite effectively by just heaping materials into a pile, you may prefer to control your pile by confining it to a structure. Here are just a few suggestions for structures—you may come up with a design that better suits your style. Just remember to make the structure at least 3 feet (90 cm) long, wide, and high, or 3 feet (90 cm) in diameter for round structures, to get the right mass of materials for good decomposition.

Wire Cages   Wire cages have the advantage of being inexpensive and portable. You can create a circle of inexpensive wire-mesh fencing, tying the ends together with wire or twine. The finer the mesh, the less compost will fall through the holes. Or you can devise a semicircle of fencing, using metal fence supports (usually called U-posts) to help it keep its shape. When it's time to turn the pile, it's easy to just remove the wire, set it up next to the original pile, and fork the compost back into the empty bin.

Bins   For a very sturdy bin, you can use cinder blocks to build a three-sided structure. Lay the blocks so the holes face the sides, not the top and bottom, so the pile gets more air. If you lay spaced boards or suspend a layer of fine wire mesh between the first and second layers of blocks, air can reach the pile from the bottom.

You can also make a wooden bin; put a door on the front if you wish. Wood-slatted snow fencing is another option for the sides.

If you have room, consider making a multiple-part bin. That way, you can turn the compost from the first bin into the second and start a new pile in the first. Or you can put quick-decaying materials in one and slower stuff in the other.

Garbage Cans   To compost in a small area, put compost materials in a large plastic, rubber, or metal garbage can that has several holes punched in the sides and bottom. Support it on bricks to keep it off the ground so excess fluid can drain out.

Compost bins can be attractive as well as functional—use locally available materials to make your own.

Picking the Right Site

The organisms that will break down organic wastes into compost need the same conditions as soil microorganisms: warmth, air, and moisture. In cool climates, putting your pile in a sunny spot can encourage decomposition; in hot climates, a shaded spot can keep temperatures from getting too hot.

You'll also want to choose a well-drained site or elevate the pile with blocks, wire, or boards; a waterlogged compost pile is as "dead" as waterlogged soil. You'll also add air each time you turn or fluff the pile with a pitchfork.

The organisms do need some moisture, though, so try to keep the pile evenly damp. If you are working with dry ingredients, spray the pile with water as you build it, so it feels about as moist as a wrung-out sponge. Some gardeners cover the completed pile with a tarp to keep it from drying out in hot weather. (This is also a good idea in very wet weather so the water doesn't leach out all of the nutrients.) In dry or windy areas, you may even need to water the pile every week or so during the decomposition process to keep it at the ideal moisture level. Or, if you're not in a hurry for finished compost, just let the pile sit until the rains come again.

Keep a container in your kitchen to collect compostable food scraps.

Compost Ingredients

Besides warmth, air, and moisture, compost organisms also need the right food. To encourage the fastest decomposition, you need to balance high-carbon materials with high-nitrogen ingredients. High-carbon materials tend to be brown and dry; think of dead leaves, old stems, pine needles, sawdust, or straw. High-nitrogen materials are often green and juicy—like kitchen scraps, grass clippings, and spoiled fruit. Finely chopped materials will break down more quickly, since there's more surface area for the microorganisms to attack.

What kinds of things don't belong in a compost pile? Meat scraps, fats, oils, and bones decompose very slowly and may attract animals to your pile. Woody prunings and thick stems will take a long time to break down unless you chop or shred them. Don't add cat, dog, or human feces, which may carry diseases. Also avoid adding weeds with seeds, perennial weeds with spreading roots (like Canada thistle), and diseased plant material, at least until you've perfected your hot-composting skills. In normal piles, these

As it breaks down, compost provides a small but steady supply of nutrients for great plant growth.

materials will survive the composting process, and you'll end up spreading weeds and disease spores through your garden as you spread the compost.

Building Your Compost Pile

If you just pile up a bunch of organic material without watering, turning, or balancing the carbon and nitrogen, a small population of soil organisms will slowly decompose the stuff in the pile over a year or two (assuming you add no new material). This approach is called cold composting. If you have the room to create several piles, and if you're not in a hurry

---

Compost Troubleshooting

If your compost pile isn't looking like it should, check the list below to see what the problem is.

• Pile doesn't heat up. Add more high-nitrogen material. If the pile is dry, add water. Try turning the pile.

• Pile smells bad. Add more high-carbon material. If the pile is too wet, turning may help add more air.

• Finished compost is covered with seedlings. If your compost doesn't heat up enough, seeds of weeds and other plants may survive. Either avoid adding materials with seeds or make sure they're in the center of a hot compost pile.

• Material doesn't break down. Woody stems, prunings, and dry leaves are often slow to break down; try shredding or chopping them into smaller pieces before adding them to a new pile. Adding more high-nitrogen ingredients can help balance these high-carbon materials.

If your compost supply is limited, spread a ¹/₂-inch (12 mm) layer around each plant and top that with another mulch.

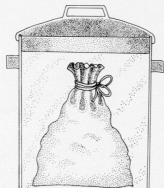

Brew a Bucket of Compost Tea

Compost tea is a liquid fertilizer made by soaking compost in water. Put a shovelful of compost into a bag made of cheesecloth or burlap. Tie the bag closed and suspend it in a garbage can, bucket, or watering can filled with water. Keep it covered for a few days. Once it has steeped, use the liquid to drench the soil at the base of plants you want to fertilize. Or dilute the liquid with water until it is the color of weak tea, then spray it on plant leaves. Because the nutrients are dissolved in water, the plants can take them up immediately for a quick burst of energy. (Reuse the "tea bag" several times, then add the soaked compost to the garden.)

for finished compost, this approach may be for you.

On the other hand, if you do fluff and water and balance carbon and nitrogen, the organisms will reproduce rapidly, creating so much activity that the pile will heat up. This is hot composting, and the temperatures in the pile can reach 160°F (71°C) or more, especially in the center. These temperatures can be hot enough to kill off weed seeds, roots, and disease organisms, if you put these in the middle of the pile.

To get the right balance of carbon and nitrogen, you can either build alternating layers, or just mix up roughly even amounts of each type of ingredient. Make sure the finished pile is evenly moist. Within a few days, the pile should feel warm. When it begins to cool again, turn the pile. Depending on your energy level, you can turn it every few days or only once every week or two. Frequent turning will encourage faster decomposition; you can have finished compost in as little as 2 weeks, though 4 to 8 weeks is more common.

Using Compost

How do you know when your compost is ready? It depends on what you want to use it for. If you want to improve the soil's structure and ability to hold water and nutrients, let the organic matter break down until the original materials are almost unrecognizable. Then work the compost into new beds as a soil amendment.

If you want a bulky material to use as a mulch, interrupt the breakdown earlier, while you can still identify some of the components. Because undecayed organic matter causes a growth spurt among the soil microorganisms, tying up some nutrients for a while, it's best to put on new or slightly aged compost after the fall harvest, so it can cook down more before spring.

Vegetables and Annuals   Work in a 2- to 3-inch (5 to 7.5 cm) layer of finished compost before planting; keep a 1- to 3-inch (2.5 to 7.5 cm) layer around plants during the season as a mulch. Protect the soil over winter with a layer of partially finished compost.

Lawns   Work in finished compost before seeding a new lawn. Top-dress established lawns with a thin layer of finished compost in late fall or early spring.

Trees, Shrubs, and Perennials   Mulch plants with a 1- to 3-inch (2.5 to 7.5 cm) layer of finished compost in early spring and/or late fall. Cover the compost with another mulch, if desired.

Spray the leaves of your crops once or twice a month with compost tea to provide extra nutrients for good growth.

Mulches keep soil from splashing onto plants during heavy rain, so flowers stay cleaner and plants stay healthier.

Straw mulches are too coarse for flower gardens, but they are great for protecting vegetable and fruit plantings.

Making the Most of Mulch

Mulching is the practice of covering the soil surface with a material that smothers weeds and prevents moisture from evaporating quickly from the soil. There are many different materials you can use as mulch—organic materials, such as pine needles or bark chips; inorganic materials, like old carpeting or black plastic; or even a living mulch of plants. In this section, you'll find out about the various advantages of mulch and how you can use mulch to improve soil, promote great plant growth, and reduce garden maintenance.

Why Mulch?

Like compost, mulch is one of those "miracle" materials that no garden should be without. If you already use mulches, you may not realize all of the different ways you can manage them to improve your garden. If you've never used mulches before, you may be surprised to learn all the things they can do for you.

Weed Control The right mulch can just about eliminate the need to pull out weeds. Mulches prevent sunlight from reaching the soil surface, so most weed seeds can't sprout.

Leave a small mulch-free zone around plant stems.

Only the most tenacious perennials poke through, such as yellow nutsedge (*Cyperus esculentus*), Canada thistle (*Cirsium arvense*), or johnsongrass (*Sorghum halepense*). If weeds germinate on top of the mulch, they're easy to pull or hoe out of the loose material.

Temperature Control By covering the soil surface, mulches reduce the amount of sunlight and wind that reach the soil, so water evaporates from the soil more slowly. And the soil stays cooler, so the roots stay cooler—a big help in the heat of the summer. In fall,

Cocoa shells make an attractive mulch, though they break down quickly and need to be reapplied during the season.

Bark chips are a good-looking and long-lasting mulch for permanent plantings, like perennial beds and groundcovers.

Chopped leaves and grass clippings make great mulches, and you probably can get them from your own garden.

a mulch can help hold in soil warmth, encouraging good root growth on perennials, shrubs, and trees. During winter and spring freeze-and-thaw cycles, mulch can keep soil temperatures even, protecting perennial plants from being pushed out of the soil.

Adding Organic Matter   A mulch can also add organic matter to the soil, improving its structure and fertility and encouraging a healthy population of microorganisms. For permanent plants like trees and shrubs, mulching may be the only way to increase soil organic matter levels. Mulches can also provide a slow-release source of nutrients to all kinds of plants.

Good Looks   Finally, mulches can make a garden more attractive, especially a new area where the plants have yet to fill in. And when it rains, a mulch keeps soil from splashing onto the leaves and flowers or nearby paved surfaces or buildings.

Picking the Right Mulch for You

When choosing a mulch, consider how long you want it to last, how attractive you want it to be, what's available, and how much you want to spend.

In general, the bigger the pieces in the mulch, the longer it lasts. Soil organisms can digest a blade of clipped grass pretty quickly, but they might need a year or two to chomp through a pine bark nugget. And juicy materials, like compost,

deteriorate faster than woody ones, like newspaper. So if you want a long-lasting mulch, as you might around trees and shrubs, choose bark nuggets or another big, woody material. If you want a mulch that deteriorates in a season, as you might, to improve the soil in a vegetable garden, go with something small and juicy like grass clippings or apple pomace.

Also think about how you want the mulch to look. Some materials, like compost, cocoa hulls, and chopped leaves, look good enough to surround the flowers in front of the house. Others, such as straw and newspapers, are best left in the back among the vegetables.

The final considerations are how available the mulch is and how much it costs. Some mulches, such as newspaper and grass clippings, are easy to come by and inexpensive. Others, like bark mulch, are also easy to come by but cost a few dollars a bag. And some mulches, such as mushroom compost, cocoa shells, apple pomace, and pecan shells, are often limited to areas where there are mushroom farms, candy factories, cider presses, and pecan groves. Ask other gardeners in your area about their favorite mulches—where they get them, how much they cost, and how they use them.

To learn more about the benefits, disadvantages, sources, and application guidelines for 15 common organic mulches, see "Organic Mulches," starting on page 52.

The Pros and Cons of Plastic Mulch

If you want a mulch to add organic matter to your soil, you need to use an organic mulch. In some cases, though, inorganic mulches—like black plastic—have a place in the garden, too. The trick to managing a plastic mulch is understanding what it will and won't do.

Black plastic can work wonders in the vegetable garden. It is great for warming up the soil in spring, getting heat-loving crops like melons and sweet potatoes off to a good start.

It will also keep the fruits of low-growing plants like strawberries and cucumbers clean. And it will hold in soil moisture and prevent weed growth.

On the down side, plastic mulch doesn't add organic matter. It will also prevent most rain from wetting the soil, so you'll need to apply extra water by hand at the base of each plant or else use a drip irrigation system. Black plastic may heat the soil too much for cool-loving crops like lettuce; either remove the mulch or cover it with a lighter mulch, like straw. And don't use black plastic around permanent plants, like trees and shrubs. Along with the other disadvantages, it will encourage shallow, easily damaged roots, eventually weakening and killing the plants.

To use black plastic, lay a sheet over a bed of prepared soil, and weight down the edges with soil or rocks. Use a knife or bulb planter to cut planting holes, and sow seeds or set transplants in through the holes. Take up and store the plastic over winter; it should last several seasons this way.

Applying Mulch Properly

Whatever material you choose, you want to apply it deeply enough to control weeds, but not so deep that it smothers the roots of your garden plants. How deep that is depends on the plant, how dense the mulch is, and how well aerated the soil is. Start by putting a 1- to 2-inch (2.5 to 5 cm) layer of mulch around flowers and vegetables and a 3- to 4-inch (7.5 to 10 cm) layer around trees and shrubs. Always weed the area before you apply any mulch. If new weeds pop through the mulch, pull them out and add another inch (2.5 cm). As the mulch breaks down, add more to keep it at the right level.

Managing Your Mulch

Given all the helpful things a mulch can do, it's hard to admit that mulches have some drawbacks. The trick is to be aware of potential problems so you'll know what to do to avoid them.

Possible Pest Problems   Soil-dwelling pests such as slugs and snails love the moist shady hiding place a mulch provides. If these pests are abundant enough to cause serious damage, you need to rake off the mulch for a while. Always avoid piling mulch against plant stems; otherwise, you'll encourage insects and animal pests, as well as diseases. Keep a mulch-free zone at least a few inches (centimeters) wide around all plants.

Keeping Soil Too Cool   In spring, or year-round in cool climates, a thick layer of mulch may keep the soil too cool, slowing root growth and inhibiting the activity of soil microorganisms. Rake off mulches in spring until the soil warms up (usually in late spring or early summer). In cool climates, keep mulches on

If you live in an area where pine needles are plentiful, try them as a mulch for either flower or vegetable gardens.

Groundcovers can act as a living mulch in ornamental plantings: They protect the soil and keep it cool.

If your flowers are attacked by slugs or snails, consider reducing or eliminating mulch—it's a hideout for pests.

the thin side. You may also want to use dark mulches, like compost, that will trap heat; light-colored mulches such as straw can reflect heat and keep soil too cool for warm-season crops such as melons and sweet potatoes.

Disturbing Soil Nutrient Balances Sometimes adding mulch can stimulate a rapid increase in soil microorganisms, which may temporarily tie up some soil nutrients. This is especially true with high-carbon mulches like wood chips and sawdust; the soil microorganisms will scavenge all of the available nitrogen in the soil and your plants will suffer. If you add high-carbon mulches, fertilize the soil first with a high-nitrogen material like bloodmeal or chicken manure, so your plants won't suffer from a nutrient deficiency. Or apply a thinner layer of high-carbon mulch over a layer of more balanced material, such as compost, leaf mold, or grass clippings. Used alone, high-carbon mulches *are* good for paths, since they can help starve out any weeds that pop up.

Grow vetch as a living mulch under late crops of broccoli.

Grow a Living Mulch

With a little planning, you can even use living plants as mulch. The easiest approach is to space your plants so they just touch as they mature. The plant canopy will block sunlight from reaching the soil, keeping the soil cool and moist, and inhibiting weed seed germination. The drawback to this technique is that it can take several weeks for plants to grow big enough to shade the soil. In the meantime, you'll have to weed and water more frequently. This technique doesn't add much organic matter either, so you'll have to supply it some other way.

In the vegetable garden, try growing a living mulch in paths and under taller crops. Low-growing white clover makes a great groundcover, protecting the soil while adding nitrogen and organic matter; its white flowers also attract beneficial insects. Vetch is another useful crop for a living mulch. Try sowing it around late crops of broccoli or brussels sprouts about 1 month after planting those crops. When you harvest the crops, the vetch will remain to protect the soil over winter. Turn it under before sowing your spring crops.

ORGANIC MULCHES

COMPOST

Homemade compost is a cheap, fertile mulch and soil amend-
ment. Top finished compost with a coarser mulch, like wood
chips, or mix it with sawdust for bulk.

BENEFITS: Compost is an ideal soil-building mulch for
vegetable gardens, flower beds, or tree and shrub
plantings. The dark color absorbs heat, helping to
warm the soil in spring. Compost is also a good
bottom layer for nitrogen-depleting mulches like
woods chips.

DRAWBACKS: Fully decomposed compost is too fine to
smother weeds. Partially decomposed compost can
trigger a burst of activity in soil organisms, which
ties up some nutrients that plants need. Seeds and
disease organisms may survive the composting
process. If you toss diseased or seed-containing
fruits, vegetables, flowers, or weeds into your pile,
save the compost for use as a soil amendment.

SOURCES: You can make your own compost from fallen
leaves, grass clippings, kitchen scraps, and other
plant debris; see "Creating Great Compost" on
page 44 for details. If you don't have a compost
pile, you can buy compost by the bag or in bulk at
garden centers, but it's relatively expensive. Many
municipalities have community composting pro-
grams, and they make compost available to resi-
dents for no charge or a small fee.

HOW TO USE: Apply a layer 1–3 inches (2.5–7.5 cm)
thick around vegetables and flowers, keeping it at
least 1 inch (2.5 cm) from the stems to prevent rot.
Apply partially decomposed compost over garden
beds in fall to finish breaking down before spring.

LEAVES, SHREDDED

A layer of shredded leaves over an inch (2.5 cm) or so of compost makes an attractive, nutrient-adding mulch for ornamental gardens during the growing season.

BENEFITS: Shredded leaves form a lightweight, insulating mulch well suited to protecting perennials, bulbs, roses, herbs, and late-season root crops (like carrots and parsnips) during the winter. Leaves are readily available, generally free for the asking.

DRAWBACKS: Shredding can be dusty and time-consuming work. (It's worth it, though. Shredded leaves won't blow away or pack down like whole leaves; they break down more quickly, too.)

SOURCES: Collect leaves from your yard; ask your neighbors for theirs, too, if you need more. Although you can buy leaf shredders, your lawn mower is probably the best shredding tool around. Rake the leaves into a long, low pile and run a power mower over it, catching the leaves in a bag. Or make a tall round pile and tilt the mower back, then onto the pile. If you have a push mower, spread the leaves in a thin layer on a paved area and run the mower back and forth over them.

HOW TO USE: Apply a layer 4–6 inches (10–15 cm) thick any time of year. Shredded leaves also make a good amendment when worked into the soil; they add nutrients and organic matter. The fresh leaves might inhibit the growth of some plants as they break down in the soil, so you may want to work in a mixture of leaves and compost in fall; the area should be fine for planting by spring.

LEAF MOLD

Leaf mold—which is basically just broken-down leaves—is a nutrient-rich mulch that you can use like compost. Leaves are readily available and usually free for the asking or raking.

BENEFITS: Leaf mold is not particularly decorative, but it's a fine choice for vegetable gardens and bush and tree fruits. If you want to use this mulch in ornamental beds, you may want to cover it with something more attractive, like shredded bark or wood chips.

DRAWBACKS: It can take several years for leaves to decompose into leaf mold. A leaf-mold mulch can keep the soil too wet if the site is poorly drained or if you live in an area with frequent rain.

SOURCES: Rake leaves from your yard; you may want to ask your neighbors for their leaves, too. Some cities also make leaves available. Don't collect them from backyard woodlots or public lands; they are needed there to feed the trees.

To make leaf mold, shred the leaves first by raking them into piles and running the lawn mower over them. Then dump the shredded leaves in a pile; you may want to build a wire bin to contain them. To make the leaves break down quicker, keep them moist and fluff them with a pitchfork every month or so. The leaf mold is ready when it's soft and crumbly.

HOW TO USE: Add up to 3 inches (7.5 cm) of leaf mold to the soil surface as a mulch. If you live in a rainy area or your soil isn't well drained, wait to mulch until early summer (when the soil has warmed up and dried out a bit).

HAY AND STRAW

Hay and straw are great summer mulches for the vegetable garden; their loose texture makes them excellent winter mulches for roses and perennials.

BENEFITS: Hay and straw are good mulches for vegetables, cutting gardens, fruit plantings, and other areas where appearance isn't important. The light color reflects sunlight, helping to keep the soil cool and moist.

    Hay is higher in nitrogen than many mulches, so it breaks down faster, and its decomposition doesn't tie up soil nutrients. Straw lasts longer than hay. It is usually free of weed seeds and is often used to keep newly seeded lawns moist between waterings.

DRAWBACKS: Straw is tough and high in carbon, so soil organisms may draw nitrogen and other nutrients from the soil as they work to digest the straw; this can affect plant growth. Hay can contain weed seeds; you may want to compost it first. Because neither material is very dense, some weeds can pop through. Both materials also are quite flammable.

SOURCES: You can sometimes get hay or straw from garden centers but more often from local farmers or farm-supply stores. Old or spoiled hay and straw is just as good as fresh bales.

HOW TO USE: Apply a layer of loose hay or straw 4–6 inches (10–15 cm) thick. Add more hay several times during the season to keep the layer thick and reduce weed sprouting. You may want to put down a layer of compost or leaf mold under a straw mulch to prevent any nutrient deficiencies while the straw breaks down. If you use hay or straw as a winter mulch, apply it after the ground freezes.

GRASS CLIPPINGS

Unlike many other mulches, grass clippings contain balanced amounts of carbon and nitrogen, so they generally don't draw nitrogen from the soil as they break down.

BENEFITS: Gardeners use both dry and fresh grass clippings as mulch around all kinds of plants to hold in soil moisture and add organic matter. Fresh grass clippings add a little nitrogen to the soil. Clippings are readily available and easy to apply.

DRAWBACKS: Fresh clippings stimulate microorganisms so much that the clippings can get hot and damage tender plant stems. When the weather is humid, fresh grass clippings can mold and smell, especially if applied too thickly to allow adequate air circulation. (To avoid molding, compost or dry the clippings first, or apply in thin layers under another mulch, like wood chips.) Grass that has gone to seed or contains weed seeds can create a weed problem in the garden.

SOURCES: Collect grass clippings from your lawn or your neighbor's. If you're not sure whether the lawn has been treated with pesticides or herbicides, avoid using the clippings or compost them first.

HOW TO USE: If you're applying fresh clippings, add a layer about 1 inch (2.5 cm) thick around established plants (less in humid conditions). Leave at least 1 inch (2.5 cm) of unmulched soil around each plant. You can double the mulch thickness for dried clippings. Sprinkle a thin layer over seeded rows until seedlings are 3–4 inches (7.5–10 cm) tall; then apply more to bring the level up to an inch or two (2.5–5 cm). Replenish as necessary.

BARK, SHREDDED

Shredded bark is composed of narrow strips of bark from hardwood or softwood trees. Use it alone or as a covering for less-attractive mulches like newspaper or pomace.

BENEFITS: Shredded bark is an attractive, natural-looking mulch for ornamentals like trees, shrubs, roses, and perennials or on paths in the vegetable garden. The small pieces break down faster than chunks or chips, so they provide more organic matter. Shredded bark generally costs less than bark chunks and about the same, or slightly more than, wood chips.

DRAWBACKS: Bark is high in carbon, so soil micro-organisms draw nitrogen and other nutrients from the soil as they break the bark down. Shredded bark can float out of plant beds in a downpour, especially on a slope. Fresh shredded cypress mulch may be toxic to seedlings, so it should be composted first. Shredded bark is far less effective than bark chunks for smothering weeds.

SOURCES: You can find shredded bark at the same places as bark chunks and chips: garden and home centers. Other possible sources include sawmills or paper mills.

HOW TO USE: Spread a 3–4-inch (7.5–10 cm) layer around trees, shrubs, and perennials or on pathways. If you use shredded bark to mulch vegetables and annual flowers, you may want to rake off the mulch at the end of the season and reapply it after planting the following year.

BARK CHUNKS

Sometimes called nuggets, these attractive pieces of bark are about 3 inches (7.5 cm) in diameter. Because they're so large and woody, they last a long time—for years in some climates.

BENEFITS: Of the various sizes of bark mulches, chunks are the best for weed control. The coarse texture of bark chunks also discourages big growth spurts in the soil microorganism population that can tie up soil nutrients. Water penetrates the loose mulch easily, and the chunks stay in place.

DRAWBACKS: Bark chunks are relatively expensive, although you'll pay less if you can find a source that sells them in bulk. They decompose slowly, so you'll have to put a finer organic material—like compost, leaf mold, or grass clippings—under them if you want to improve the soil.

SOURCES: Bark chunks are widely available; look for them at garden centers, discount stores, hardware stores, and even grocery stores.

HOW TO USE: Bark chunks are a good ornamental mulch for trees and shrubs or for covering the spaces between plants in a new shrub or perennial bed. Spread the mulch to a depth of about 3–4 inches (7.5–10 cm).

WOOD CHIPS

Wood chips are small pieces of bark and wood from chipped or shredded tree limbs. Since they're fairly long-lasting, wood chips are used mostly for permanent plantings and pathways.

BENEFITS: Wood chips make a decorative, weed-suppressing mulch. Use coarse chips on paths and around trees and shrubs; finer chips (about 1 inch [2.5 cm] square) are good around roses and perennials. Wood chips are relatively long-lasting, but they break down faster than bark chunks, adding more organic matter to the soil. They are also less expensive than bark chunks.

DRAWBACKS: Wood chips are high in carbon, making soil organisms draw nitrogen and other nutrients from the soil as they work to digest the chips; this can affect plant growth. Bags labeled "wood chips" can contain wood other than bark, including leftovers from furniture manufacturers or other industries; ask about the source before you buy. Freshly chipped wood needs to sit for a few months before you use it since the tree might have contained natural substances toxic to young plants.

SOURCES: Wood chips are sold by the same sources as bark chunks, as well as by some municipalities. Avoid mulch that smells like vinegar or ammonia; sour mulch can be highly acid and toxic to plants.

HOW TO USE: Spread wood chips to a depth of about 3–4 inches (7.5–10 cm) around trees and shrubs or in the spaces between plants in a new perennial or shrub planting. Apply a layer of compost, leaf mold, or grass clippings under the chips to avoid nutrient deficiencies.

COCOA BEAN SHELLS

Cocoa bean shells are good for keeping the soil moist and suppressing weeds; plus, they add nitrogen, phosphorus, and potassium to the soil as they break down.

BENEFITS: Cocoa bean shells (also called cocoa hulls or cocoa mulch) are clean, weed-free, and have an appealing smell of bitter chocolate when first applied. These lightweight and easy-to-handle shells are used as an ornamental mulch around trees, shrubs, roses, and perennials. The rich, brown color is very attractive.

DRAWBACKS: Because the fresh hulls are lightweight, they can blow around in windy areas. After several months, the shells can pack down in wet weather. They also mold easily, although mixing them with sawdust can help prevent this problem. Because they last a long time, cocoa bean shells aren't ideal for vegetable gardens or annual beds where you'll be digging frequently. They can be expensive if there's no local source.

SOURCES: If you have a chocolate factory in your area, you can buy inexpensive cocoa hulls at local garden centers. If you don't, you can order them from some garden-supply catalogs for a premium price.

HOW TO USE: Apply a layer 1–2 inches (2.5–5 cm) thick. Wet the shells after applying them to help them settle and prevent them from blowing.

MUSHROOM COMPOST

Mushroom compost (also known as mushroom soil) is the spent manure that's left after mushrooms are harvested. It's a good source of organic matter, as a mulch or soil amendment.

BENEFITS: Mushroom compost is a fine-textured mulch that will add organic matter and nutrients to your soil. Use it as you would compost.

DRAWBACKS: Unless you apply a thick layer, mushroom compost doesn't suppress weeds as effectively as a coarser mulch. If the mushroom grower applied pesticides to the crop, traces may remain in the mushroom compost; ask before you buy. Fresh material may contain a high amount of salt; old, weathered piles may have accumulated weed seeds.

SOURCES: Buy mushroom compost from mushroom farms or garden centers in mushroom-growing areas. If possible, look for mushroom compost that has been aged for a few months.

HOW TO USE: Apply a layer about 2 inches (5 cm) thick, keeping a mulch-free zone at least 1 inch (2.5 cm) in diameter around the base of each plant. If you can only get fresh mushroom compost, consider composting it first, or apply it to the vegetable garden the fall before planting. You can turn it under the following fall. Like regular compost, mushroom compost is a good bottom layer for carbon-rich mulches like wood chips, shredded bark, straw, or sawdust.

NEWSPAPER

Newspaper is a cheap and effective weed-suppressing mulch. To keep it from blowing around, cover it with a decorative mulch such as cocoa bean shells, bark, or shredded leaves.

BENEFITS: Sheets of newspaper create a barrier that weeds have a tough time breaking but water can easily pass through. Newspaper breaks down slowly, adding organic matter to the soil. It's inexpensive and readily available.

DRAWBACKS: Deciding how thick to make the layer can be tricky. If it's too thin, it won't last as long as you want and weeds will pop up. Too thick and you have to pull it up at the end of the season if you want to turn the soil or add fertilizer. Newspaper mulch isn't very attractive, and it's flammable.

SOURCES: Use your old stack of newspapers or ask your neighbors for theirs. Black-and-white newspaper is fine, and colored newspaper is usually safe to use as well; avoid using the glossy, highly colored advertising inserts because the inks may contain toxic materials.

HOW TO USE: Lay sheets of paper on the soil surface (wait for a calm day, if possible!) and weigh them down with grass clippings, soil, compost, garden trimmings, or some other material to keep them from blowing away. Start by making the layer ten sheets thick; reapply if the layer breaks down before the season ends. Shredded newspaper also makes a good mulch. If you have access to shredded paper, water it thoroughly after applying it, and tramp it down to keep it from blowing away.

PINE NEEDLES

Pine needles, also called pine straw, are used widely in the southern United States. They make a good-looking, light-weight mulch for shrubs, trees, and perennials.

BENEFITS: Pine needles are long-lasting, weed-free, and attractive, with a fresh, piney smell. They can help increase soil acidity, so they make an ideal mulch for acid-loving plants like blueberries, azaleas, and rhododendrons; they are also good for mulching other shrubs, flowers, and trees. The light weight prevents pine needle mulch from smothering plants and lets water and air reach the soil.

DRAWBACKS: Pine needles are quite flammable, making them a fire hazard during droughts.

SOURCES: You can collect pine needles from your yard or a neighbor's yard, or buy them by the cubic foot (30 cubic cm). Don't collect them from the forest; leave that organic matter to fertilize the trees. Some sources do collect the pine needles they sell from public lands; ask your supplier about the source, and avoid needles that were collected from the forest.

HOW TO USE: Apply a layer 2–4 inches (5–10 cm) thick to the soil surface, especially around acid-loving plants.

POMACE

Apple pomace is the pulp that remains after apples have been pressed for cider. You can use it fresh, but it's easier to apply once it has been composted.

BENEFITS: Apple pomace is a good one-season mulch for vegetable and flower gardens, especially if it's composted and mixed with straw or another dry material. Pomace contains phosphorus and potassium.

DRAWBACKS: Apple skins can contain pesticide residues that may be toxic in large amounts. Pomace attracts flies and ants, and it can smell sour as it decays. Because it's soggy straight from the press, compost fresh pomace first, preferably with an absorbent material such as shredded leaves.

SOURCES: Commercial cider makers sell or give pomace away. Wineries may produce a similar by-product, called grape pomace.

HOW TO USE: Fresh apple pomace makes a dense mulch, so apply a thin layer, no more than about 1 inch (2.5 cm) thick. Composted pomace can be used like other types of compost: Alone, in a 1–3-inch (2.5–7.5 cm) layer, or in a thin layer under high-carbon mulches like sawdust, wood chips, or shredded bark. Fresh or composted pomace also is a good source of organic matter when worked into the soil.

SAWDUST

Fresh or aged sawdust is an excellent choice for mixing with or laying over compost, grass clippings, mushroom soil, and other nutrient-rich mulches.

BENEFITS: Aged sawdust mulch is fine for vegetables, small fruits (like blueberries), and ornamental plantings; it's also a good mulch on paths. Although it is fine-textured, it is good at deterring weeds, especially if it's mixed with another mulch.

DRAWBACKS: Sawdust is so high in carbon that you'll need to add extra nitrogen, unless it has been composted or aged for a year or two (until it turns gray). Sawdust can blow around when dry or wash away during heavy rains. It is also quite flammable.

SOURCES: Collect sawdust from your building projects. Sawmills, furniture factories, paper mills, and lumberyards may sell or give it away. Don't use sour-smelling sawdust; it may harm plants.

HOW TO USE: It's a good idea to compost sawdust before adding it to the soil surface, both to lower the carbon to nitrogen ratio and to give any toxic substances in the wood a chance to leach out. Then spread 1–2 inches (2.5–5 cm) on the soil surface.

PEAT MOSS

Peat moss is not desirable as a mulch. Freshly applied dry peat can blow around, and it is flammable. Compared to other mulches, peat is also quite expensive.

BENEFITS: Although many gardeners automatically equate peat moss with mulch, it's generally not a good use of peat (see "Drawbacks" below).

DRAWBACKS: Some peat moss, especially that from Louisiana, is acid enough to burn plants. Dry, loose peat moss will absorb lots of water, so all but the heaviest rains may not even reach the soil before the water is trapped by the mulch. If peat moss dries out, it may crust over and shed water rather than absorbing it.

SOURCES: Garden centers, home centers, and discount stores are a few common sources for peat moss. It is usually sold in plastic-wrapped bales of various sizes.

HOW TO USE: Peat moss is better used in small amounts as a soil amendment or potting mix ingredient rather than in large amounts as a mulch. Whenever possible, choose compost, shredded leaves, or some other mulch that can provide all the benefits of peat moss without the drawbacks. For more information on using peat moss as a soil amendment, see the Peat moss entry on page 88.

Work legumes like vetch into the soil to add organic matter and extra nutrients for later crops.

Growing Cover Crops and Green Manures

If you have a spot where nothing is planted for at least part of the year—in the vegetable garden or perhaps in an annual flower bed—try growing a cover crop or green manure to protect and improve the soil.

What's the Difference?

Basically, there isn't much difference between cover crops and green manures. Both groups include the same kinds of plants, such as clover, winter rye, and buckwheat. The real difference is why you grow those plants. A green manure is a crop you plant right where you want more organic matter. At some point in its life, you dig the crop into the soil and let the roots, stems, and leaves feed soil organisms and improve the soil structure. A cover crop does the same thing, except that it's also used to keep soil from washing or blowing away in between crops or before the main crop—usually vegetables—fills in.

You can see it's a fine distinction and not all that critical, so it's okay if you forget which is which. The important thing to remember is that they both add organic matter to the soil. For the rest of this section, we'll use the term green manure, since that is really what you're growing for the purpose of adding organic matter.

Why Grow Green Manures?

Like mulches and compost, green manures can also do great things for your soil and your plants. The roots loosen the soil and provide additional organic matter while the crop is growing. If you grow a legume (like clover or vetch) as a green manure, it adds nitrogen to the soil. A green manure can choke out weeds and protect the soil from the eroding effects of wind and rain. Green manures take up nutrients that might otherwise wash from bare soil, then slowly return the nutrients to the soil as they decay. Last, but not least, they provide lots of organic matter when you dig or till them into the soil.

Picking the Right Green Manure Crop

When you are deciding which green manure crop to grow, you need to know when and where you will grow it. Some manure crops, like winter rye and hairy vetch, are planted in the fall and turned under in the spring. Others, like buckwheat and oats, will go from seed to usable growth in just a few weeks during the growing season. Also consider the growing conditions your

Ryegrass is a good choice for a fast-growing green manure. Work it into the soil before it sets seed.

garden has to offer. Most green manure crops grow best in well-drained soil, but some, like alsike clover, can take wetter conditions. Leguminous crops (like clovers, alfalfa, and soybeans) usually prefer soils with a pH near neutral; others tend to be more adaptable to soils with a lower pH. You'll find out the specifics on 15 different crops in "Cover Crops and Green Manures," starting on page 62.

You can plant a grass or legume as a green manure or a mix of both. Grasses are better at adding organic matter and stimulating earthworms, while legumes add more nitrogen. If you plant a legume, you'll need to spread a commercially available inoculant on the soil or treat the seed with it before planting. The inoculant contains the nitrogen-fixing bacteria that live in legume roots. Not all inoculants are the same, so make sure you buy the kind that works best for your particular crop. Alfalfa and sweet clover share one type; true clovers, peas and vetch, lespedezas, and soybeans all use different strains of bacteria. Your supplier should be able to get you the right kind or sell you a mixture that will work for several crops.

Working green manures into the soil is easy when the plants are young; older plants make for difficult digging.

Green Manure Warnings

Green manures can do good things for your garden, but they can be a problem too if you don't handle them right. The key to success with green manures is working them in at the right time. If you wait too long to work in winter rye in spring, it will keep regrowing and can get to be a weed. And if you let buckwheat go to seed before you turn it under, you may see it sprouting up through your crops for seasons to come (though they're not a serious pest). To avoid problems, see "Cover Crops and Green Manures," starting on page 62; it will give you guidelines on how and when to work in each crop.

Many gardeners have trouble working the tough stems of mature green manures into the soil. If this is a problem for you, try turning the manure crop in at an earlier stage, when the growth is a little softer.

If you live in the arid West, be aware that the manure crop can deplete the soil's water reserves that following crops will need. Eventually, though, the extra organic matter from the green manure will help these dry soils hold more water for all your crops.

Growing and Handling Green Manures

To plant a green manure, prepare a fine soil bed by raking the surface. You can wait until you've harvested existing plants or sow it a few weeks before the season ends. Scatter the seed as evenly as you can, then rake them in and tamp the soil down. If you don't get rain while the seeds are germinating, water to keep the seedbed moist until the seedlings are up and growing; a light mulch will help, too.

When you till or dig in the crop depends on the results you want. If you turn under the manure crop when it's still young and tender, it will decompose quickly and add a lot of nutrients. If you wait until it's older (but before it sets seed), it will add more organic matter; it will also be tougher to dig in.

It will be easier to work the green manure crop into the soil if you cut the stems first. Use a scythe to chop the leaves and stems, or mow with a sickle-bar mower; if the crop is short, a regular or mulching mower can do the job. Let the cut material dry for a few days before working it in. If you covered only a small area with a green manure, you can turn it under with a spade. For a larger area, use a rotary tiller. Tough plants such as old alfalfa may require a few passes. You should always allow at least a few days—maybe a week or two if you've turned in very coarse material—between turning under the manure crop and planting your garden.

Avena sativa   Gramineae

OATS

Late-summer sowings of oats will die over winter, forming a thick layer of soil-protecting mulch. Dig or till in the remains in early spring, about 2 weeks before planting.

HOW TO USE: This quick-growing annual grass is especially good as a temporary groundcover when you're establishing a perennial cover crop like clover. Or try a summer sowing of oats as a living mulch crop for late-season vegetables like broccoli and brussels sprouts.

BEST CLIMATE AND SITE: Oats grow best in cool, moist climates, although they can adapt to gardens in many parts of the United States. Oats are not as cold-tolerant as other small grains. They grow best in full sun.

SOIL AND MOISTURE NEEDS: Oats adapt well to many different soil conditions, but they prefer evenly moist soil. They grow well in soil with average fertility and can tolerate a wide range of pH.

GROWING GUIDELINES: You can plant oats just about any time during the growing season for use as a green manure. The seeds will germinate best when the soil is cool, though. Use 4 ounces (120 g) per 100 square feet (9.3 sq m) or 2¹/₂ pounds (1.2 kg) per 1,000 square feet (93 sq m). Scatter the seed over the bed and rake it in. Firm the seedbed after planting. For the most nutrients, mow the crop when plants are 4–6 inches (10–15 cm) tall, then till them under. Older stands will provide more organic matter when worked into the soil, but be sure to get them before the seed heads form; otherwise the oats may self-sow.

| *Fagopyrum esculentum* | Polygonaceae | *Glycine max* | Leguminosae |

BUCKWHEAT

SOYBEANS

Buckwheat's hollow stems and tender leaves break down quickly when worked into the soil, adding organic matter. The blooms attract beneficial insects, including bees.

If you haven't grown soybeans in the past 4 years, apply an inoculant (a powder of beneficial bacteria available from many seed suppliers) to the seed before planting.

HOW TO USE: Use this fast-growing, broad-leaved annual to quickly smother summer weeds. Buckwheat is a great cover crop to fill garden spaces that will be open for a few weeks during the season (between spring harvest and summer planting, for instance). It can provide usable green manure growth in as fast as 5–6 weeks. The hollow stems and tender leaves break down easily, building organic matter and adding phosphorus to the soil.

BEST CLIMATE AND SITE: Buckwheat is adapted to many climates and withstands hot weather well. It cannot take frost. It prefers full sun.

SOIL AND MOISTURE NEEDS: Grows in a wide range of soil conditions, including infertile and acid soil.

GROWING GUIDELINES: Sow in spring or summer, after the last frost when the soil is warm. Plant 5 ounces (150 g) per 100 square feet (9.3 sq m) or 3 pounds (1.35 kg) per 1,000 square feet (93 sq m) in the spring or summer. Broadcast the seed over the prepared bed and rake it in. Dig plants in by hand when they are 4–6 inches (10–15 cm) tall for the most nutrients. Or, for more organic matter, wait until later in the summer; mow the plants just after they begin to bloom, let the material dry for a day or two, then work it into the soil. Don't allow plants to set seed; they'll self-sow prolifically.

HOW TO USE: This annual legume is a good summer cover crop or green manure, especially for adding nitrogen to poor soil where other legumes fail. As a green manure, soybeans are often grown with a grass such as buckwheat. Soybeans are also useful as a cover crop under corn plantings.

BEST CLIMATE AND SITE: Soybeans prefer sunny sites and a warm climate, but they can take some shade and adapt to many parts of the United States.

SOIL AND MOISTURE NEEDS: Soybeans grow best in well-drained soil, with a moderate amount of moisture. Unlike many other legumes, they will tolerate poor drainage and somewhat acid soil. They can also withstand some drought.

GROWING GUIDELINES: Sow in spring or early- to mid-summer; seeds germinate best when the soil is warm. Plant 3–5 ounces (90–150 g) of soybean seed per 100 square feet (9.3 sq m) or 2–3 pounds (0.9–1.35 kg) per 1,000 square feet (93 sq m). Cover with $^1/_2$–1 inch (12–25 mm) of soil. If you have a tiller, you can wait until fall to turn the plants under. Otherwise, you may want to dig the plants in at an earlier stage (ideally when flowering); the older stems and roots can be tough and hard to work in by hand. Either way, you may want to mow the tops first to make the job easier.

Lespedeza spp.   Leguminosae

LESPEDEZA

Lespedezas are excellent green manure and cover crops for improving poor soil, especially where soil is too acid or temperatures are too warm for red clover or alfalfa.

HOW TO USE: Korean and striate lespedeza (*Lespedeza stipulacea* and *L. striata*) are annuals primarily used for late-summer and fall cover; they die off over winter. Perennial sericea lespedeza (*L. cuneata*) has a deep root system, making it good for controlling erosion and adding organic matter.

BEST CLIMATE AND SITE: Grown primarily in the eastern half of the United States, from central Pennsylvania to northern Florida, and as far west as Nebraska. Korean lespedeza is most common in the northern part of this range; striate and sericea lespedeza are more widely grown in the South. Lespedezas thrive in a sunny position.

SOIL AND MOISTURE NEEDS: Korean and striate lespedezas tolerate eroded, acid soil. Sericea lespedeza is good for nutrient-poor, acid soils where few other crops thrive. Lespedezas are fairly drought-tolerant, but they prefer areas with ample rainfall.

GROWING GUIDELINES: If you haven't grown lespedeza on a given site within the past 4 years, apply an inoculant (a powder of beneficial bacteria available from many garden centers and seed suppliers) before planting. Sow in late winter to late spring at a rate of 1^1/$_2$ ounces (45 g) per 100 square feet (9.3 sq m) or 1 pound (450 g) per 1,000 square feet (93 sq m). Broadcast the seed over the bed, rake it in, and firm the seedbed. Dig or till plants under in late summer or fall, before they set seed.

Lolium multiflorum   Gramineae

ANNUAL RYEGRASS

Annual rye is a good fast-growing green manure crop for building soil organic matter. Dig or till plants in before they flower and set seed to prevent self-sowing.

HOW TO USE: Annual ryegrass (also known as Italian ryegrass) is useful when you need a green manure that germinates quickly, loosens the soil, and prevents soil erosion. In Southern states, it's often seeded with perennial lawn grass to hold the soil in place while the perennial grass fills in. Annual rye often dies out during cold weather, but some of the seed may come up for the next 2–3 years.

BEST CLIMATE AND SITE: Annual rye overwinters in the central and southern United States. It won't survive winters in the North, but even after it dies, its thick growth makes a fine winter cover crop. Annual rye needs a sunny site.

SOIL AND MOISTURE NEEDS: Annual rye germinates well in cool soil. It does well in a wide range of soil pH and textures but prefers loamy or sandy soil. It can take some drought, although it grows best in evenly moist soil.

GROWING GUIDELINES: Plant in spring to late summer; late sowing is best if you want a winter cover crop. Scatter 1^1/$_2$–3 ounces (45–90 g) of seed per 100 square feet (9.3 sq m) or 1–2 pounds (450–900 g) per 1,000 square feet (93 sq m). Rake the seed into the soil, then firm the seedbed. Dig or till the crop under when it is 4–6 inches (10–15 cm) tall, before it flowers and sets seed. Or, for winter cover, wait until spring to mow the dead tops and dig or till in the crop.

| *Medicago sativa* Leguminosae | *Melilotus* spp. Leguminosae |

ALFALFA

SWEET CLOVER

If your soil is well drained and of average fertility, it's hard to beat alfalfa for adding nitrogen. Alfalfa's deep roots also help draw nutrients up from the subsoil.

HOW TO USE: Plant this perennial legume where it can grow as a green manure or cover crop for at least two seasons. Or plant it in a permanent spot and harvest the stems and leaves for use as a nutrient-rich organic mulch. It's high in protein, minerals, and vitamins.

BEST CLIMATE AND SITE: Alfalfa grows throughout the United States. It's better adapted to dry regions than red clover.

SOIL AND MOISTURE NEEDS: For best growth, alfalfa needs a deep, well-drained soil with a pH near neutral and adequate amounts of phosphorus, potassium, calcium, and sulfur. It is drought-tolerant, especially once established.

GROWING GUIDELINES: The first time you grow alfalfa on a given site, treat the seed with an inoculant (a powder of beneficial bacteria available from many garden centers and seed suppliers) before planting. Sow in spring in the North, in late summer elsewhere. Plant 1 1/2 ounces (45 g) per 100 square feet (9.3 sq m) or 1 pound (450 g) per 1,000 square feet (93 sq m). Mow and till 2-year-old stands under in spring when new growth reaches 4–6 inches (10–15 cm) tall. Or wait until summer, when plants are in full bloom, then cut and compost or mulch with the tops and till in the stubble.

Sweet clover is good for improving infertile or disturbed soil that isn't acid. The decomposing residues add phosphorus, nitrogen, and lots of organic matter to the soil.

HOW TO USE: White sweet clover (*Melilotus alba*) can be annual or biennial; yellow sweet clover (*M. officinalis*) is a biennial. Some seeds may not germinate until the second or third year, so don't be surprised to see sweet clover popping up among future crops. Choose a different cover crop if this will be a problem.

BEST CLIMATE AND SITE: Sweet clover adapts well to a variety of climates, but it is grown mostly in the central United States from Canada to Mexico and in the Great Lakes states.

SOIL AND MOISTURE NEEDS: Sweet clover requires well-drained soil with an alkaline or near-neutral pH. It won't tolerate acid soil. Sweet clover is moderately to highly drought-resistant, although evenly moist soil will produce the best growth.

GROWING GUIDELINES: Sow in spring or summer; seed germinates best in cool soil. If you have not grown sweet clover or alfalfa on the site within the past 4 years, treat the seed with an inoculant (a powder of beneficial bacteria available from garden centers and seed suppliers) before planting. Scatter seed at a rate of 3/4–1 1/2 ounces (21–45 g) per 100 square feet (9.3 sq m) or 1/2–1 pound (225–450 g) per 1,000 square feet (93 sq m). Rake it in, then firm the seedbed. Dig or till in annual white sweet clover in fall before plants set seed. Wait until the spring of the second year, when plants are about 6 inches (15 cm) tall, to turn under biennial types.

| *Secale cereale* | Gramineae | *Sorghum sudanense* | Gramineae |

WINTER RYE

SUDANGRASS

Winter rye plants have a vigorous root system that protects the soil from erosion. The roots and lush spring growth also can add plenty of organic matter.

Sudangrass, also known as grass sorghum, is closely related to grain sorghum (Sorghum bicolor). Sudangrass and sorghum sudangrass hybrids grow quickly in warm weather.

HOW TO USE: Winter rye is an easy-to-establish, reliable winter cover crop for just about any kind of soil. The plants have a vigorous root system that protects the soil from erosion, and the roots and lush spring growth add lots of organic matter to the soil. Since it grows early in the spring and produces toxins that kill seedlings, winter rye is ideal for smothering weeds. Like other grasses, its fibrous root system and succulent leaves add organic matter.

BEST CLIMATE AND SITE: Rye adapts to most U.S. climates; it is very winter-hardy. It grows best in full sun.

SOIL AND MOISTURE NEEDS: Winter rye prefers well-drained soil with a near neutral pH, but it is adaptable. It is quite drought-tolerant.

GROWING GUIDELINES: Plant in the late summer or fall at a rate of 4 ounces (120 g) per 100 square feet (9.3 sq m) or 2½ pounds (1 kg) per 1,000 square feet (93 sq m). Till plants under in spring. The decaying residues of winter rye release substances toxic to other plants. This makes it good for weed control, but it also means you can't sow small-seeded crops such as lettuce and radishes right after turning the rye under. Transplants and large-seeded crops generally aren't affected, but you may want to wait 3–5 weeks before planting to be on the safe side.

HOW TO USE: Grow this tall annual grass as a summer cover crop to choke out weeds. The dense root system makes this grass well suited for erosion control. Sudangrass also reduces the number of nematodes in the soil and adds a lot of organic matter as a green manure.

BEST CLIMATE AND SITE: Sudangrass thrives in warm weather; for that reason, it's most commonly grown in warm, dry southern and central states, where legumes and other cover crops don't thrive. Sudangrass needs full sun for best growth. It can tolerate considerable drought, but it produces the best growth with adequate rainfall.

SOIL AND MOISTURE NEEDS: Sudangrass survives drought well, but it performs better with more water, especially in the Southwest. It adapts well to alkaline or poorly drained soil.

GROWING GUIDELINES: In spring to summer, when the soil is warm, plant 1½–3 ounces (45–90 g) per 100 square feet (9.3 sq m) or 1–2 pounds (450–900 g) per 1,000 square feet (93 sq m). Scatter the seed over the bed and rake it in. When plants reach 4–6 inches (10–15 cm) tall, mow the tops and till or dig them into the soil. Wait 3–5 weeks before planting your main crop; otherwise, the decomposing residues may inhibit plant growth.

Trifolium hybridum	Leguminosae

ALSIKE CLOVER

Alsike clover is a low-growing perennial that tolerates poor drainage and acid soil better than most legumes. It thrives in cool climates with ample moisture.

HOW TO USE: Use this low-growing, short-lived perennial legume as a green manure to add nitrogen and organic matter to heavy, wet, or acid soil. Grow it alone or in a mix with grasses and other legumes for better soil coverage.

BEST CLIMATE AND SITE: Alsike clover is best adapted to the northern United States, primarily Oregon and the Great Lakes states, where the climate is cool and moist. Choose a sunny spot for best growth. It is more cold-tolerant than red clover.

SOIL AND MOISTURE NEEDS: Alsike clover prefers loamy, evenly moist soil with a pH near neutral, but it will adapt to wet and acid soil better than most clovers. It doesn't tolerate drought well.

GROWING GUIDELINES: Sow in spring or late summer; seed germinates best when the soil is cool. If you haven't grown clover on the site within the past 4 years, treat the seed with an inoculant (a powder of beneficial bacteria available from many garden centers and seed suppliers) before planting. Sow $^3/_4$ ounce (21 g) per 100 square feet (9.3 sq m) or $^1/_2$ pound (225 g) per 1,000 square feet (93 sq m). Scatter the seed over the bed, rake it in, and firm the seedbed. Turn plants under in fall or early spring.

Trifolium incarnatum	Leguminosae

CRIMSON CLOVER

Crimson clover has a strong root system that provides excellent erosion control. Grow this annual legume alone or in combination with annual ryegrass or hairy vetch.

HOW TO USE: Try crimson clover as a living mulch under tall vegetables (like corn) or in bramble patches and orchards. It's often left in place over winter.

BEST CLIMATE AND SITE: Crimson clover is most commonly grown in the southeastern United States, from the Gulf states (except Florida) north to southern Illinois. It also grows on the Pacific coast. It tolerates shade and, compared to other clovers, grows well at low temperatures.

SOIL AND MOISTURE NEEDS: Crimson clover grows in either sandy or well-drained clayey soil if the pH is near neutral. The germinating seeds and young seedlings need to stay moist. Plants thrive with a good supply of phosphorus and potassium.

GROWING GUIDELINES: Sow between midsummer and early fall, when the soil is warm; the farther north you are, the earlier the planting time. If you haven't grown clover on the site within the past 4 years, treat the seed with an inoculant (a powder of beneficial bacteria available from many garden centers and seed suppliers) before planting. Scatter $^1/_2$ ounce (15 g) of seed per 100 square feet (9.3 sq m) or 1 pound (450 g) of seed per 1,000 square feet (93 sq m). Rake the seed in, then firm the seedbed. Turn the crop under in fall or early the next spring; you may want to mow the tops first. Wait 2–3 weeks before planting your next crop.

| *Trifolium pratense* Leguminosae | *Trifolium repens* Leguminosae |

RED CLOVER

WHITE CLOVER

Red clover tolerates some acidity and low fertility but thrives in fertile soil with a pH near neutral. Mow plants as soon as they flower to prevent reseeding.

Low-growing white clover spreads rapidly, making it useful as a living mulch between and under row crops or as a cover crop in permanent plantings, like orchards.

HOW TO USE: Red clover is a biennial or perennial legume that is useful as a cover crop or green manure. As it matures, it stays more tender than alfalfa, so it's usually easier to dig in. The flowers are popular with bumblebees. Red clover can be grown alone or in a mix with grasses and other legumes.

BEST CLIMATE AND SITE: Red clover is most commonly grown in the northeastern, northern central, and Pacific Northwest states, where there are moderate winter and summer temperatures. It can withstand some shade.

SOIL AND MOISTURE NEEDS: Red clover requires good drainage but doesn't tolerate drought. It especially needs moisture while becoming established.

GROWING GUIDELINES: Sow seed in the spring in the northern United States, from Tennessee north. In the South, sow in late summer to grow it as a winter annual. If you have not grown clover (any species of *Trifolium*) on the site within the past 4 years, treat the seed with inoculant (a powder of beneficial bacteria available from many garden centers and seed suppliers) before planting. Sow $^3/_4$–1$^1/_2$ ounces (21–45 g) of seed per 100 square feet (9.3 sq m) or $^1/_2$–1 pound (225–450 g) per 1,000 square feet (93 sq m). Rake lightly to cover, then firm the seedbed. Keep moist until seedlings emerge. Turn plants under in fall or spring.

HOW TO USE: Grow a cover crop or green manure of white clover to add nitrogen and other nutrients to the soil and to smother weeds. This fast-spreading legume is usually grown for at least a full year, from spring to spring. The blooms attract honeybees and other beneficial insects.

BEST CLIMATE AND SITE: White clover grows almost anywhere, with the exception of deserts, the hot tropics, and extremely cold regions. It does best where the weather is cool and moist. White clover will tolerate shade, though sun encourages more vigorous growth.

SOIL AND MOISTURE NEEDS: This crop prefers well-drained clayey or loamy soil, but it performs better in wet clay soil than most other clovers. It needs a pH near neutral, as well as good supplies of calcium, phosphorus, and potassium.

GROWING GUIDELINES: Sow seed in spring or summer. If you haven't grown clover on the site within the past 4 years, treat the seed with an inoculant (a powder of beneficial bacteria available from many garden centers and seed suppliers). Scatter $^1/_4$ ounce (7 g) of seed per 100 square feet (9.3 sq m) or $^1/_4$ pound (110 g) per 1,000 square feet (93 sq m). Rake to cover, then firm the seedbed. Dig or till the crop under before it blooms, unless you're using it as a permanent cover crop; then mow as needed to keep plants from setting seed.

| *Trifolium repens* var. *latum* | Leguminosae | *Vicia* spp. | Leguminosae |

LADINO CLOVER

Ladino clover is a tall-growing variety of white clover. Although it is technically a perennial, ladino clover may be killed by low winter temperatures in cold-climate gardens.

HOW TO USE: This tall variety of white clover usually dies during the winter, so you can more easily turn it under in the spring than regular white clover. It also produces more organic matter than white clover. It is good as a cover crop or green manure.

BEST CLIMATE AND SITE: Ladino clover grows all over the United States, but it thrives in cool, moist conditions.

SOIL AND MOISTURE NEEDS: Ladino clover prefers evenly moist, well-drained soil with a pH near neutral, but it can adapt to wet, droughty, or acid conditions.

GROWING GUIDELINES: Plant in early spring in the North or in late summer in the South. If you haven't grown clover on the site within the past 4 years, treat the seed with an inoculant (a powder of beneficial bacteria available from many garden centers and seed suppliers) before planting. Scatter ³/₄ ounce (21 g) of seed per 100 square feet (9.3 sq m) or ¹/₂ pound (225 g) per 1,000 square feet (93 sq m). Rake the seed lightly into the soil, then firm the seedbed. Dig or till plants under in fall or spring; you may need to mow the tops first.

VETCHES

Most commonly grown vetches are vining annual legumes; grow them alone or with grasses like oats or winter rye. Mature growth can be tough, so mow before digging or tilling.

HOW TO USE: There are several species, including hairy vetch (*Vicia villosa*) and common vetch (*V. sativa*). Grow hairy vetch as a winter annual to add nitrogen and organic matter to any well-drained or droughty soil. Vetch also makes a great living mulch under late-season crops like broccoli and cauliflower.

BEST CLIMATE AND SITE: Vetches grow anywhere in the Unites States. Hairy vetch is the only one hardy enough to be a winter annual in the North—the others must be planted in the spring.

SOIL AND MOISTURE NEEDS: Hairy vetch grows in most soil types, while common vetch needs fertile, loamy soil. All prefer well-drained soil and are drought-tolerant.

GROWING GUIDELINES: Sow hairy vetch in fall and other vetches in early spring. If you haven't grown vetches or peas on the site within the past 4 years, treat the seed with an inoculant (a powder of beneficial bacteria available from many garden centers and seed suppliers) before planting. Scatter 3 ounces (90 g) of seed per 100 square feet (9.3 sq m) or 2 pounds (900 g) per acre (0.4 ha). Rake to cover the seed, then firm the seedbed. Turn under hairy vetch in spring, other vetches in fall.

UNDERSTANDING FERTILIZERS

In many ways, those who call themselves organic or natural gardeners believe the same things about gardening as those who don't. Both, for example, agree that choosing plants adapted to the soil in which they'll grow makes life easier than trying to nurture something exotic. Both recognize that digging in clay soil when it's wet is a bad idea.

One topic they disagree on is fertilizer. Organic gardeners use plant and animal products as well as ground rock minerals, while non-organic gardeners use synthetic fertilizers. Gardeners who use synthetic fertilizers sometimes argue that plants can't tell the difference between nitrogen that comes from a synthetic source and the nitrogen in manure—and they're right. Nitrogen is nitrogen, whatever the source. The difference is how soil organisms, not plants, respond to the two sources of nutrients.

For soil organisms, organic fertilizers are a food source. It takes them a while to digest most organic fertilizers, so the nutrients in them become available to plants slowly. For organic fertilizers to work, there must be a healthy population of soil organisms.

The nutrients in synthetic fertilizers dissolve quickly in the water in the soil. They are so concentrated that they kill many soil organisms. Without a healthy population of microorganisms to convert nutrients to a form they can use, plants become dependent on synthetic fertilizers. When the microorganisms are out of balance, the

breakdown of organic matter is interrupted, soil structure can suffer, and your plants may not grow as well.

For all of these reasons, it makes sense to use organic fertilizers. This chapter covers all the basics you need to know for choosing and using organic fertilizers effectively. In "What Is a Fertilizer?" on page 72, you'll learn about the different kinds of organic materials that can supply nutrients to your plants. "Nitrogen for Lush Leaves" on page 74 tells about the importance of nitrogen to your plants and how you can supply it. In "Phosphorus for Roots and Fruits" on page 76, you'll learn what this nutrient does for your plants and about the different sources of phosphorus that you can apply. "Potassium for Healthy Growth" on page 78 covers the role of this nutrient in plant growth and tells how you can add it to your soil. "Other Necessary Nutrients" on page 80 covers the remaining nutrients that your plants need to grow and the various ways you can supply them.

When it is time to purchase your nutrient materials, read "Buying Organic Fertilizers" on page 82 to make sure you are getting the right product for your particular needs. "Applying Organic Fertilizers" on page 84 tells about the different ways you can add these materials, depending on the form they're in. If you're not sure what material to use, see "Organic Fertilizers and Amendments," starting on page 86; you'll learn how and why to apply 19 different organic materials, along with suggested sources.

Fertilizing is one part of gardening where more is not necessarily better. Many plants thrive with small but regular doses of fertilizer; others—like coreopsis—actually grow and flower best without extra nutrients.

What Is a Fertilizer?

Perhaps the appeal of synthetic fertilizers comes from the limited choice. You go to the store, you buy a bag of something with a picture of the right plant on the front, and you go home. On the other hand, there are enough organic fertilizers that choosing the right ones might seem confusing.

Fertilizers or Amendments?

The first step to choosing the right organic material is knowing the difference between a true fertilizer and a soil amendment. Fertilizer is a material that contains significant amounts of the chemical elements that plants need to grow, like nitrogen, phosphorus, and potassium. It may also contain material that improves the soil, such as organic matter. But its primary function is to add nutrients. Bloodmeal, bat guano, and greensand are examples of organic fertilizers.

An amendment is a material that improves the soil physically—usually its structure or drainage—or enhances microbial activity. It may contain some nutrients, but not enough to be called a fertilizer. Compost, grass clippings, lime, and peat moss are examples of soil amendments.

The material you use depends on what effect you want. Fertilizers are useful for correcting specific nutrient deficiencies and for providing a general nutrient boost during the growing season. Amendments are important for long-term soil health, since they add organic matter and humus. Work these in before planting, or use them as mulches, but don't count on them to provide enough nutrients to support heavy-feeding plants like vegetables. Using a balance of fertilizers and amendments will help ensure your plants have all the nutrients they need and help build soil humus as well.

Understanding Plant Nutrients

The materials that plants require to grow are called essential elements. Three of the essential elements plants need—carbon, hydrogen, and oxygen—come from the air. The rest come from the soil.

The essential elements supplied by the soil are divided into two groups—macronutrients and micronutrients (also known as trace elements). Macronutrients include the primary nutrients—nitrogen, phosphorus, and potassium—and, in smaller amounts, the secondary nutrients—sulfur, calcium, and magnesium. Micronutrients include iron, molybdenum, manganese, zinc, chlorine, boron, copper, and nickel.

Plants use relatively large amounts of the macronutrients, much as humans use a lot of carbohydrates, proteins, and fats. They use smaller quantities of the micronutrients, much as humans need small amounts of vitamins and minerals. The difference in the amount plants use doesn't indicate a difference in how important the element is. All are essential, and a lack of one affects how effectively plants can use the others. That's why balancing soil fertility is so important for good plant growth.

Cosmos doesn't need lots of nutrients for good growth; too much fertilizer leads to weak stems and fewer flowers.

Making compost is a great way to recycle lawn and garden trimmings, and it provides a free source of nutrients.

When you dig a green manure crop into the soil, it adds both nutrients and organic matter as it breaks down.

A light dose of compost or balanced organic fertilizer will go a long way toward meeting your plants' nutrient needs.

Natural Nutrient Sources

While there are many kinds of organic fertilizers and amendments to choose from, just about all of them fall into a few basic categories.

Rock Powders   As the name suggests, rock powders are rocks pulverized to a fine powder. Reducing the rocks to such small pieces makes it easier for soil microorganisms to get at the minerals that make up the rock. The minerals in rock powders become available to plants very slowly. The same kinds of rock mined in different areas are fairly standard in the percentage of nutrients they contain. Granite meal and rock phosphate are examples of rock powders.

Manures   Animals eat plants, and their solid waste contains the undigested organic matter and minerals from those plants. Some fresh animal manures, like horse manure, are so high in nitrogen that they burn plants; you'd either want to compost these manures before adding them or work them into the vegetable garden in the fall after harvest. Composted manure, because it contains less nitrogen than fresh manure, is a more balanced source of nutrients. Manure is also a good source of organic matter.

Unlike rock powders, the amounts of nutrients in manures varies, depending on the type of animal and what it has been eating. Manure from farm animals such as horses and cows is most common, but you can also buy the manure of crickets, worms, bats, zoo animals, and other creatures. All can be valuable, as long as you know what you are applying and what effect it's likely to have on your plants.

Green Manures   Green manures are grasses and legumes that you grow and then work into the soil to add organic matter and nutrients. For more information on growing and using green manures, see "Growing Cover Crops and Green Manures" on page 60.

Compost   Compost is decaying and decayed plant waste—kitchen scraps, fallen leaves, grass clippings, shredded paper, and so on. The nutrient balance in the compost depends on what you add to the compost pile. Well-made compost contains a small but balanced source of plant nutrients, as well as lots of organic matter. Once compost breaks down all the way, to black, crumbly humus, it's more of a soil amendment than a fertilizer. See "Creating Great Compost" on page 44 for details on making and using compost in your garden.

Dried Animal Parts   The dried blood and ground bones of animals that have become human food are used as fertilizer. These products are called meals—as in bloodmeal, bonemeal, and fish meal. Their nutrient content can vary widely, depending on what has been included and how it has been handled. "Organic Fertilizers and Amendments," starting on page 86, offers details on these materials.

In the vegetable garden, grow clover as a green manure crop; it will release nitrogen when you work it into the soil.

Nitrogen for Lush Leaves

Nitrogen is one of the three primary macronutrients that plants take up from the soil. If you've ever fertilized a lawn, you know what a quick, dramatic effect nitrogen has: It helps make plants a deep green color and stimulates leafy growth.

Nitrogen is probably the nutrient you'll have to add most often, since it easily washes out of the soil. Nitrogen makes up less than 1 percent of the soil, and most of that is bound in organic matter. It is slowly released and converted to a form plants can use, which is dissolved in the water held between soil particles. Unlike many nutrients, the form of nitrogen dissolved in the soil solution has a negative charge. Because soil colloids—the tiny particles of clay and humus—are also negatively charged, they can't hold nitrogen, and it leaches readily from the soil. That's why nitrogen is often in short supply, especially in quick-draining sandy soils or in those where it's removed by vigorously growing plants.

Noticing Nitrogen Imbalances

Plants that lack nitrogen are stunted and grow poorly. Their leaves are pale or yellow, especially the older, lower leaves. Many plants will show symptoms of nitrogen deficiency when they begin to set fruit because the demand for nutrients is particularly high at that time.

Adding extra nitrogen to beans and peas can actually reduce your harvest.

When plants lack nitrogen, they can't use other nutrients well and may also show symptoms of other nutrient deficiencies. Also, other problems can mimic nitrogen deficiency. For example, overwatering can make leaves turn yellow, and a nematode infestation can cause stunting. Consider all of these possible causes when diagnosing plant problems.

An excess of nitrogen can be as much of a problem as a lack of nitrogen. Too much nitrogen can cause flowering or fruiting plants, such as nasturtiums and tomatoes, to form lush, leafy, deep green growth at the expense of blooms or fruit. This leafiness generally isn't a problem with crops grown for their leaves, such as lettuce. However, the lush growth encouraged by excess nitrogen can make any plant more susceptible to diseases and insects. Plus, tall plants with too much nitrogen have weak stems and can fall over easily.

Since nitrogen leaches out of the soil so readily, excess nitrogen is seldom a problem. Just be cautious when applying high-nitrogen fertilizers, like fresh horse or poultry manures or bat guano. Remember, just because a little fertilizer is good, that doesn't mean that a lot is better!

Adding Extra Nitrogen

You can add nitrogen to the soil in several ways. If you have a naturally fertile soil, it's enough to just add compost or manure each year to replace the nitrogen that plants remove. These balanced materials will provide a steady supply of nitrogen to growing plants throughout the season.

If your plants need additional nitrogen, you can use a more concentrated

For nasturtiums, extra nitrogen can promote leaves at the expense of flowers.

Lupines belong to the same family as peas and beans. Like their relatives, lupines seldom need extra nitrogen.

source. Depending on the fertilizer you choose, the nitrogen may be available right away, but it may only last a short while or be released gradually over a long period. See "Organic Nitrogen Sources" for specific suggestions of materials you can add.

Growing a green manure crop of clover, alfalfa, lespedeza, or some other legume is a useful way to add extra nutrients to the soil in your vegetable garden. Legumes host beneficial soil bacteria on their roots. These bacteria draw nitrogen gas from air in the soil and convert it to a form that both they and the plants can use. When you work legumes into the soil, the decaying roots release nitrogen that other plants can absorb.

Yellowing leaves are a good clue to a nitrogen deficiency, although other imbalances can cause similar symptoms.

Organic Nitrogen Sources

Here are a few organic materials that are particularly good nitrogen sources.

- **Alfalfa meal** is ground alfalfa hay. It contains about 5 percent nitrogen and also contributes potassium.
- **Bloodmeal** contains 13 percent nitrogen. Besides being a good nitrogen source, it is sometimes used to repel deer and rabbits.
- **Cottonseed meal** contains 6 percent nitrogen as well as some phosphorus. It is often used on acid-loving crops, like blueberries. Some organic gardeners avoid cottonseed meal because it is heavily treated with pesticides.
- **Fish emulsion** is made of fish by-products dissolved in water. It is about 5 percent nitrogen. Spray it on the leaves or water it into the soil at the base of the plant.
- **Fish meal** consists of dried, ground fish parts; it's a balanced fertilizer that contains 5 percent nitrogen, 3 percent phosphorus, and 3 percent potassium.
- **Guano** is aged, dry bird or bat droppings that have been mined from roosts and caves. It varies from 10 to 15 percent nitrogen. Because it contains calcium, it raises the soil pH.
- **Legumes,** which include alfalfa, clovers, peas, and beans, have nitrogen-fixing bacteria growing in bumps, or nodules, on their roots. These bacteria can take nitrogen from the air and convert it into a form plants use. In exchange for that service, the bacteria draw carbohydrates from their host. Perennial legumes such as alfalfa and clovers fix the most nitrogen, much more than beans or peas do. If you add nitrogen to legume crops, you'll discourage them from fixing nitrogen, defeating your purpose. You can include legumes in a crop rotation or grow them as a green manure.

Phosphorus is important in creating a great crop, from healthy roots to strong stems and good seed formation.

Phosphorus for Roots and Fruits

Like nitrogen, plants need large amounts of the primary element phosphorus. Plants use phosphorus to flower, fruit, and form seeds. Phosphorus helps crops mature, counteracting the effects of too much nitrogen. Roots need phosphorus to develop, especially the fibrous roots that spread out to absorb water and nutrients. Phosphorus makes stems strong and improves the quality of vegetables; it also improves disease resistance.

Identifying Phosphorus Imbalances

Plants that lack phosphorus often turn purple under the leaves and on the stems, especially at the base. The plants, including the roots, are stunted. Their stems are skinny and brittle. The leaves may have yellow streaks, and fruit sets and matures late.

Plants grown in extremely acid or alkaline soils often show signs of phosphorus deficiency. Deficiencies are also common in seedlings when the soil is cold, since the microorganisms that release much of the phosphorus are not very active. Soils high in aluminum are often low in available phosphorus. A

lack of phosphorus also limits how well your plants absorb other nutrients, especially nitrogen.

Excess phosphorus is rarely a problem. But if you add too much phosphorus fertilizer, it may limit plants' supplies of iron, manganese, or zinc.

Supplying Phosphorus

Most soils are naturally low in phosphorus, and most of the phosphorus that is there isn't available, especially in soils that are very acid or alkaline. In soils with an extreme pH, the phosphorus reacts with chemicals in the soil, such as iron, calcium, aluminum, and manganese, to create compounds that plants can't absorb. If you add phosphorus to very acid or alkaline soil, much of it binds to these chemicals.

The first step toward making more phosphorus available to plants is to adjust the pH so it's near neutral. In acid soils, this means adding lime. In

Maintaining the soil's pH near neutral will help to keep adequate phosphorus available to your plants.

Phosphorus doesn't move much in the soil, so it's best to work it into the root zone. For perennials, shrubs, and trees, your best chance to do this is before planting.

A purplish cast to the leaves is a common sign of phosphorus deficiency, especially on seedlings.

alkaline soils, add sulfur. The pH changes slowly, so it's a good idea to test your soil once or twice each year for several years, collecting samples about the same month each time. (For more information on dealing with acid or alkaline soils, see "Gardening in Acid Soil" on page 102 or "Growing in Alkaline Soil" on page 104.)

The next step is to add a phosphorus fertilizer, both to increase the supply in the soil and to replace the phosphorus that crops remove. You'll find suggestions of some common phosphorus-supplying materials in "Organic Phosphorus Sources." Since microorganisms help make phosphorus more readily available, many gardeners add phosphorus to their compost piles rather than directly to the soil.

Because phosphorus doesn't dissolve readily, it doesn't move down through the soil. For that reason, you must put it where it's needed—in the root zone. Dig or till phosphorus-bearing fertilizers into the soil to get them into the root zone. The actual depth will vary, depending on the plant. For grass it's 2 to 4 inches (5 to 10 cm) deep, for vegetables it's about 6 inches (15 cm), and for trees and shrubs it's from near the surface to about 18 inches (45 cm) deep. This makes it important to correct major phosphorus deficiencies before planting, especially for more permanent features like lawns and trees.

When it is cold, even soil that has plenty of phosphorus may not supply the needed nutrient to your plants. In permanent plantings, rake off heavy mulches in spring to help the soil warm more quickly. In the vegetable garden, try a black plastic mulch to warm the soil before planting.

Organic Phosphorus Sources

If your soil is low in phosphorus, try one of these materials to give it a boost.

- **Bonemeal,** made from ground animal bones, has 11 percent phosphorus. Steamed bonemeal is a more available source of phosphorus than raw bonemeal. Both release phosphorus more quickly than rock phosphate.

- **Rock phosphate** is less expensive than bonemeal, but it takes longer to release its phosphorus. The more finely ground the rock, the more quickly the phosphorus is released. Rock phosphate is about 32 percent total phosphate, but only about 3 percent is available at any one time.

- **Colloidal phosphate** is clay washed from between the layers of rock phosphate. It has half as much total phosphorus as rock phosphate, with about 2 percent being available at any one time. The phosphorus in colloidal phosphate is more readily available than that in rock phosphate. Colloidal phosphate also contains about 20 percent calcium.

- **Fish emulsion and liquid seaweed** give a quick shot of phosphorus when sprayed on the plants or watered into the soil. The effect isn't long-lasting but can be a big help for young plants forming roots, plants setting fruit, and plants showing symptoms of a phosphorus deficiency.

- **Animal manures** contain phosphorus as well as nitrogen and potassium. Poultry manure has the highest phosphorus content, at about 14 percent total phosphorus. About 2 percent is available at any time.

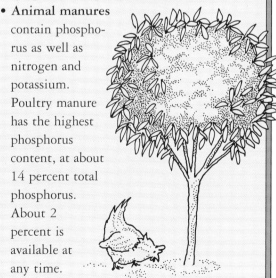

Potassium for Healthy Growth

Although potassium doesn't get as much attention as the other primary nutrients, plants use as much potassium as they do nitrogen and about four times as much as they use phosphorus. Potassium makes plants vigorous because it helps them develop strong root systems and resist disease. It regulates how plants absorb nitrogen, sodium, and calcium. Potassium also balances the tendency of nitrogen to cause leafy growth and of phosphorus to encourage fruiting. Plants use potassium in photosynthesis, and it is part of the process that moves newly photosynthesized sugars from the leaves to the roots, then converts them to starches. Because of potassium's role in forming starches, potatoes and other tubers require high amounts of this element.

Picking Up on Potassium Imbalances

If plants don't get enough potassium, they are stunted and yield poorly. Leaves develop irregular yellow splotches, starting at the bottom of the plant and working upward. In more severe cases, the leaves are dry and scorched at the edges. The symptoms worsen as the season progresses.

Take care when diagnosing a potassium deficiency because other problems have

Mulching with compost each year will provide a small but steady supply of potassium to plants.

Potassium plays a role in tuber formation, so it's particularly important for potatoes.

similar symptoms. Nematodes, for example, can also cause stunting or poor yield. Some diseases cause similar leaf splotches. Drying winds can make leaves look dry and scorched—maple trees are particularly plagued by this problem.

Excess potassium is seldom a problem under normal conditions. But if you apply too much potassium fertilizer to the garden, it can interfere with your plants' use of other nutrients.

Keeping Potassium at the Proper Level

Most soils, except those composed mostly of sand, are high in total potassium. The problem with potassium, as with phosphorus, is that much of it is unavailable. Ninety percent or more is in rock minerals such as mica and feldspar, which resist weathering.

Some potassium is loosely trapped between the microscopic layers that make up clay particles. The potassium held in these reservoirs slowly makes its way to the soil solution for plants to absorb. Some clays, such as those common in cool and dry climates, are better reservoirs than those in humid and warm climates. Clays in cool, dry regions keep more potas-

Greensand, kelp meal, and granite powder are a few good sources of potassium for your organic garden.

A good balance of soil potassium will promote strong, healthy growth in all of your crops.

Potassium deficiency often causes leaves to turn yellow with brown edges; symptoms appear on older leaves first.

Yearly applications of compost or a balanced organic fertilizer will supply most of the potassium your flowers need.

sium from washing, or leaching, out of the soil.

Fortunately, if you add potassium to the soil, it's not immediately rendered unavailable as phosphorus is. Plants can absorb it until it leaches from the soil. They can absorb it so readily, in fact, that they may take up more than they need or can use, a situation known as luxury consumption. This can interfere with the plant's uptake of other needed nutrients.

The trick to keeping potassium at the right level is to apply it twice a season, half a dose each time, rather than putting it on all at once. This method gets around both the leaching and the luxury consumption problems, so your plants get just what they need.

Some sources of potassium are more soluble than others; these are more readily available, but are more likely to wash from the soil. "Organic Potassium Sources" covers some of the best materials for adding potassium to deficient soils. Working compost into the garden before planting, or using it as a mulch afterward, will also add some potassium to the soil.

Organic Potassium Sources

Correct potassium deficiencies with any of these organic sources.

- **Granite powder** is finely ground, potassium-rich granite mined from quarries. It contains about 4 percent total potassium, which it releases slowly.
- **Greensand** is a mineral mined from ocean beds that have raised and dried over time. It's a slow-release source, with 7 percent potassium.
- **Langbeinite** (also sold as Sul-Po-Mag) is a source of quick-release potassium. It contains about 22 percent potassium. It also adds magnesium and sulfur to the soil without altering the pH.
- **Kelp meal** is dried, ground seaweed. It contains between 2 and 3 percent potassium in a relatively available form, as well as trace minerals.
- **Wood ashes** collected from stoves and fireplaces contain potassium and other minerals. Some of the nutrients are soluble enough to burn plants; for that reason, it's best to compost ashes first or let them sit out in the rain. Wood ashes are easy to overuse, so only apply them every few years. Wood ashes raise the soil pH and should not be used on alkaline soils.

Other Necessary Nutrients

Besides nitrogen, phosphorus, and potassium, plants need large doses of calcium, magnesium, and sulfur—the secondary macronutrients. They also need micronutrients to grow and thrive in your garden.

Calcium

Calcium helps plants absorb nitrogen and create proteins. Without it, new leaves and end branches emerge deformed; the upper leaves curl upward and turn yellow around the edges, then dry and fall off. The stems are hard, and the roots are brown and stubby. Blossom end rot, where the bottom of fruits turn brown or black, is a common symptom of calcium deficiency in tomatoes and peppers. Drought can cause calcium deficiency because plants can't absorb it from the soil. Excess potassium can also limit available calcium.

Limestone is the main source of calcium. Limestone also neutralizes soil acidity, making it a useful addition to acid soils but definitely something to avoid on alkaline soils. If you have alkaline soil that is calcium-deficient, add gypsum. Calcium is also in fertilizers that supply other nutrients, such as rock phosphate, bonemeal, kelp meal, and wood ashes, and in shells from oysters and eggs.

Magnesium

Magnesium is part of the chlorophyll molecule, which makes plants green and is essential for photosynthesis. Without magnesium, plants are chlorotic—the leaves are pale with dark green veins. The leaves may be brittle and curl up. Fruit matures late or not at all. Deficiencies are more common late in the season and in soils with too much potassium or calcium. You can correct a magnesium deficiency in an acid soil by adding dolomitic limestone, which contains magnesium carbonate. In alkaline soils, use Epsom salts, which is magnesium sulfate.

Sulfur

Sulfur is part of proteins that plants build. Plants with a sulfur deficiency are small, pale, and spindly. Sulfur also makes soils acid. It is rarely lacking, except in

A lack of zinc can cause leaves to turn yellow between the green veins and to roll under along the edges.

some parts of the Southeast, the Northwest, California, and the Great Plains. Adding ample quantities of organic matter will usually supply all the sulfur your plants need. To lower soil acidity, you can use sulfur dust, also known as flowers of sulfur.

Micronutrients

While plants may need pounds of the macronutrients, they need much smaller amounts of the micronutrients. These tiny amounts make diagnosing and correcting micronutrient deficiencies difficult. If you add more of a micronutrient than is needed, it can be toxic or throw off the balance of their nutrients.

Micronutrients are most often deficient in peat, muck, or very alkaline soils, although some are also limited in acid soils. In most cases, adding organic matter will supply all the micronutrients your plants need. Keeping the pH near neutral will ensure that the micronutrients are readily available. A quick solution is to spray with liquid seaweed, so the nutrients bypass the soil and go straight into the plant where they are needed.

Mottling and dead spots on leaves can be signs of magnesium deficiency.

Iron Plants use iron in chlorophyll synthesis and in enzymes and proteins. Of the micronutrients, iron is needed in the highest amount. An iron deficiency produces yellow leaves (chlorosis) with dark green veins.

Finished compost will supply a wide range of necessary nutrients to all of your garden plants.

Iron deficiencies are quite common on alkaline soils.

Manganese   Manganese (not to be confused with magnesium) plays a role in both chlorophyll and vitamin synthesis. It also helps the plant use carbon and nitrogen. Signs of manganese deficiency include blotchy leaves, fewer buds forming, buds that drop, and twigs that die back. Manganese may be deficient in soils with too much copper, zinc, calcium, or magnesium. In highly acid soils, manganese can be toxic.

Zinc   Zinc helps plants form growth hormones and plays a role in seed production and maturation. Without zinc, leaves may look mottled and may roll at the edges. Shortened spaces between leaves on the stems give plants a rosetted appearance. Excess nitrogen, copper, or aluminum can create a deficiency.

Copper   Copper helps plants make enzymes and chlorophyll. It's also used in plant respiration and to metabolize carbohydrates and proteins. The symptoms of copper deficiency are similar to those of iron deficiency. Deficiencies are common in soils with too much nitrogen, phosphorus, or zinc.

Boron   Boron is used in making proteins, moving starches and sugars up and down the plants, developing roots, forming fruit and seeds, and absorbing water. The new leaves on boron-deficient plants are black, and the shoots at the end of branches curl inward. Alkalinity and excess potassium in the soil can create a boron deficiency.

Molybdenum   Molybdenum is part of protein synthesis and nitrogen fixation. Deficient plants have curled, thick, and brittle leaves; dead buds; and fruit that is discolored and deformed. Extreme soil acidity and excess copper make molybdenum deficient.

Chlorine, Sodium, Cobalt, and Nickel   The actual functions and deficiency symptoms of chlorine, sodium, cobalt, and nickel are still being studied by scientists. So far, it's known that cobalt is involved in nitrogen fixation and chlorine improves root and top growth.

Seaweed—in its fresh form or prepared as an extract—is an excellent source of calcium and micronutrients.

Many nutrients, in varying amounts, are necessary for your plants to produce healthy growth and beautiful flowers.

For most plants, a balanced organic fertilizer applied once or twice a year will meet their needs. Spot-treat plants that have special requirements with a single-nutrient material.

immediately available nutrients to be listed, even though the total percentage of the nutrient might be higher. The nutrients in most organic fertilizers aren't very soluble, so they're released gradually. For example, rock phosphate contains about 32 percent of total phosphorus, but only about 2 percent is available at any one time. So even though the label can only claim a "2" in the NPK ratio (as in 1-2-1, for instance), the material actually contains much more phosphorus. The other 30 percent will gradually become available to your plants over the following few growing seasons.

Just because the label only gives nitrogen, phosphorus, and potassium doesn't mean the fertilizer doesn't contain other materials, too. Bonemeal, for example, is high in calcium as well as phosphorus. Because calcium raises the soil pH, you wouldn't want to apply bonemeal to an alkaline soil. Seaweed contains

Buying Organic Fertilizers

Just a few years ago, you would have had a hard time finding any organic fertilizer products at your local garden or home center. Fortunately, more and more outlets are selling a variety of commercially packaged organic fertilizers. Before you buy, it's handy to know a few things about labeling guidelines and laws. That way, you'll be sure you're getting the right fertilizer material for your particular needs.

Reading the Label

When you're in any store, faced with a row of different products, how do you tell them apart? Read the labels! To get the right fertilizer, though, it's not the ingredients or price tag that you're looking for but a series of three numbers separated by dashes. Because nitrogen, phosphorus, and potassium are the three nutrients most in demand in agricultural crop production, labeling laws require that the available percentage of each be listed on fertilizer packages. This listing is sometimes called the NPK ratio, since N, P, and K are the chemical symbols for nitrogen, phosphorus, and potassium, respectively. A bag labeled 8-5-4, for example, contains 8 percent nitrogen, 5 percent phosphorus, and 4 percent potassium. This breakdown is called the nutrient analysis.

You may notice that the nutrient analyses for organic fertilizers are lower than those for synthetic ones. That's because labeling laws allow only the

Do You Need Balance or a Boost?

A fertilizer with nearly equal percentages of nitrogen, phosphorus, and potassium is called a general-purpose, complete, or balanced fertilizer. The balance may be natural, or it may result when different materials are mixed together. A balanced fertilizer is a good choice for fertile soils when you just want to replace the nutrients plants remove.

A fertilizer may instead have one dominant nutrient. Bloodmeal's analysis, for example, is 11-0-0; it supplies only nitrogen. Use these single-nutrient fertilizers if a soil test shows that one element is particularly lacking. Check nutrient levels with a soil test each year before you add a single-nutrient fertilizer to make sure that you still need it and that you're adding the right amount.

Applying Fertilizer

Scatter dry organic fertilizer evenly over the planting bed.

Or apply the fertilizer in a ring around the base of each plant.

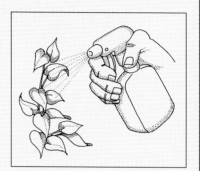

Spray liquid fertilizers on the leaves for a nutrient boost.

many trace elements as well as nitrogen, phosphorus, and potassium, which is good to know if you suspect micronutrient deficiencies. Labels don't always mention that the product supplies micronutrients, so ask the supplier or manufacturer if you have questions.

Is It Really Organic?

If you want to make sure that you're adding a truly organic fertilizer, read labels carefully before buying any product. Seeing the word "natural" or "organic" isn't necessarily as reassuring as you might hope. On fertilizer labels, "organic" may just mean that the product contains some form of carbon. The word "natural" denotes a fertilizer derived from plant, animal, or mineral sources, even if it has been manipulated in a way that most organic gardeners find unacceptable

(such as superphosphate, which is rock phosphate doused with sulfuric acid).

Read the label thoroughly, including all that small print on the back. Look for information on other materials the fertilizer contains and what it's made from. Some manufacturers are better than others in giving all the details, so shop around and ask questions.

One trick you can use to tell organic and synthetic materials apart is to look at the NPK ratio. Be suspicious if one or more of the three numbers is higher than 10, or if the three numbers added together total more than 15. Most organic fertilizers have low NPK ratios. Products with higher ratios (like 20-20-20) generally contain supplemental synthetic ingredients, such as urea and superphosphate. If you have doubts, ask the seller or the company that produces the product.

Some plants like sneezeweeds (*Helenium* spp.) don't require special fertilizer; compost provides enough nutrients.

Fast-growing annual flowers and vegetables benefit from fertilizer worked into the planting bed or scattered on the soil.

Side-dress shrubs with dry fertilizer in spring. Use a hoe or rake to lightly scratch the material into the soil.

Applying Organic Fertilizers

Exactly how you apply a given fertilizer material depends on what form it is in. Fertilizers can be solids or liquids. Solid fertilizers, which you apply dry, may be fine powders, large granules, or something in between. Fertilizers you apply wet may come as powders that you dissolve in water or as concentrates that you dilute with water.

Handling Dry Fertilizers

Dry fertilizers are, obviously, less soluble than liquid ones, so they work more slowly but last longer. You can spread a dry fertilizer evenly over a large area, a method called broadcasting. Or you can sprinkle dry fertilizer next to a plant or beside a row of plants— a technique called side-dressing. Broadcasting is for lawn fertilizers and fertilizers that are applied to an unplanted bed. Side-dressing is for established plants, either annuals that need a midseason boost or perennials. To get the nutrients to the roots faster, lightly scratch the side-dressed fertilizer into the soil, being careful not to nick roots or stems.

Fertilizer spreaders work well for evenly broadcasting dry fertilizers over large areas. For small areas, you can use a handheld rotary

Wear gloves to protect your hands when applying fertilizers.

spreader. For side-dressing, use a trowel or spade, shaking the fertilizer off the end to scatter it over the soil as you walk among the plants.

Applying Liquid Fertilizers

Since the nutrients in liquid fertilizer are already dissolved in water, they provide a quick boost to plants during the growing season. To apply a liquid fertilizer, first dissolve or dilute it according to label instructions. If you plan to spray the fertilizer solution on the leaves—called a foliar spray—you may want to add a surfactant. A surfactant is a material, usually a soap, that helps the fertilizer stick to the leaves better, giving the plant more time to absorb the liquid before it drips off. You can buy surfactants at garden centers or

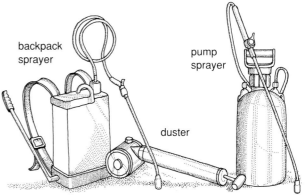

backpack sprayer
pump sprayer
duster

Adjusting Application Rates

Most fertilizers packaged for home use give application rates in useful units—teaspoons per plant, pounds per 1,000 square feet, and the like. But sometimes you may buy a material packaged for agricultural use, such as limestone, with an application rate given in pounds per acre. Unless you have a *really* big garden, you'll probably have to convert that rate into something more manageable.

Downsizing a dosage might seem like it requires an advanced degree in calculus, but in truth it only requires a pocket calculator and a few numbers. Divide the pounds of material to apply per acre by 43,560 (which is the number of square feet in an acre). That will tell you the number of pounds to apply for 1 square foot. Then multiply the answer by the number of square feet you plan to fertilize. That number is the pounds you need. If that number is so small that it would be easier to work in ounces, multiply it by 16.

Follow the application suggestions on your soil test report to get the best results from any fertilizer.

Treat small plantings with a handheld mister.

make your own by adding a drop or two of dish soap or detergent per gallon (4.5 l) of fertilizer. Don't use too much or you can damage the leaves.

Because plants close down their leaf pores when it's sunny or hot, try to apply foliar fertilizers early or late in the day or during a cloudy spell. Spray them on the tops and undersides of the leaves until the liquid runs off. A handheld mister works fine if you're only dealing with a few plants. If you're applying a liquid fertilizer to large areas, try a backpack sprayer or a hose-end sprayer. (For those of us with math anxiety, there are calibrated hose-end sprayers; you just turn the dial on the top until the arrow points to the number of teaspoons or ounces the label calls for; the unit does all the diluting for you as you apply the fertilizer.)

You can also apply liquid fertilizers to the soil at the base of plants. Before you do, water the soil if it's dry. If you're fertilizing just a few plants, you can use a sprinkling can with a perforated cover over the spout. For large areas, try the hose-end sprayer described above.

How Much Should You Apply?

Before you go out to buy and apply a fertilizer, it's smart to make sure your plants need it. It's a waste of your time and money to add unneeded nutrients, and you could actually do more harm than good. Adding too much of one nutrient can interfere with plant uptake of other essential elements. Too much lush growth from excessive fertilizing can make plants more prone to pests and diseases. Remember, if a little fertilizer is good, more fertilizer is not necessarily better!

If you are applying a complete fertilizer to give your plants a nutrient boost during the season, you can probably get away with following the application suggestions on the bag. But the safest bet is to get your soil tested by a professional laboratory; see "Taking Soil Tests" on page 23 for directions.

The results of the test should recommend amounts of particular nutrients or materials you need to add to balance the soil's fertility. If you ask for organic recommendations when you send in your sample for testing, you may or may not get the information you need, depending on the particular lab you're dealing with. If you only get suggestions for synthetic fertilizer, your local Cooperative Extension Service or garden center should be able to help you convert them to the appropriate organic materials.

Scatter dry fertilizer over flower beds in early spring while the plants are still small. Once plants cover the soil, it's hard to spread fertilizer effectively.

LIME

Both calcitic and dolomitic lime are suitable for garden use; look for labels with either of these terms or the words "ground limestone," "agricultural lime," or "garden lime."

WHAT IT IS: Lime is a general term applied to products that contain various forms of calcium carbonate. Calcitic lime is mostly calcium carbonate, with a small percentage of magnesium carbonate. Dolomitic limestone is about half calcium carbonate and half magnesium carbonate. Avoid hydrated lime, slaked lime, builder's lime, or quicklime, which are very caustic and can damage plants.

WHAT IT DOES: Lime slowly increases the pH of soil, reducing the acidity. It also adds calcium and magnesium.

HOW TO APPLY IT: Ideally, you should take a soil test to find out if your soil needs lime and how much you should use. If you know that your soil is acid, you can follow these general guidelines: Spread 6 pounds (3 kg) per 100 square feet (9.3 sq m) if your soil is clayey. Use 4 pounds (2 kg) on the same area if your soil is loamy; use 2 pounds (1 kg) on sand for the same area. Test the soil after a few years to gauge the lime's effect and add more if necessary.

Apply lime with a garden spreader, or scatter it by hand for small areas; be sure to wear heavy gloves to protect your skin. For more information on buying and using limestone effectively, see "Raising the pH" on page 103.

WHERE TO FIND IT: You can purchase lime at garden centers or through garden-supply catalogs.

SULFUR

Sulfur is one of the most effective amendments you can use to lower pH. To avoid drastic pH changes, test your soil's acidity after the first dose before applying more.

WHAT IT IS: Sulfur is a naturally occurring mineral. It is often sold as elemental sulfur, flowers of sulfur, or agricultural sulfur; it may be in the form of a powder or "prilled" (with larger particles).

WHAT IT DOES: Sulfur lowers the pH of soil by bonding with excess calcium and magnesium. Use sulfur to decrease the alkalinity of high pH soil.

HOW TO APPLY IT: In fall or winter, broadcast 1 pound (450 g) per 100 square feet (9.3 sq m) to lower the pH by one full point (for example, from 8 to 7). Mix the sulfur into the top 3 inches (7.5 cm) of soil. The more organic matter the soil has, the less it will respond, so you'll have to add more sulfur. If you need to apply more than 1 pound (450 g), make two applications: Put on half in late winter or early spring and the other half in the fall after harvest. To lower the pH around existing plants, scratch the sulfur into the soil at the base of the plant, as far out as the end of its branches. Test the soil after the first application. If the pH is still too high, make another application. For more details on using sulfur, see "Lowering Soil pH" on page 104.

WHERE TO FIND IT: Purchase sulfur at garden centers or through garden-supply catalogs.

COMPOST

Finished compost is dark and crumbly, with most of the original ingredients completely broken down; unfinished compost still has some recognizable ingredients.

WHAT IT IS: Decayed and partially decayed plant waste from the garden and kitchen, sometimes mixed with animal manure. The nutrient analysis of compost varies depending on what materials are in it and how long it has aged; it may range from 0.5-0.5-0.5 to 4-4-4.

WHAT IT DOES: Partially decayed (unfinished) compost adds nutrients and organic matter to the soil and stimulates soil microorganisms. Decayed (finished) compost primarily adds organic matter and humus, as well as some nutrients. Any compost is excellent as a general soil conditioner, helping to improve drainage in tight, clayey soil and increase water retention in loose, sandy soil.

HOW TO APPLY IT: Spread a layer of finished compost 2–3 inches (5–7.5 cm) deep on the soil surface and turn it under any time the ground isn't frozen. You can also add a handful to planting holes when transplanting. Unfinished compost is best added in fall; work it in or leave it on top of the soil so it can finish breaking down before spring digging and planting.

WHERE TO FIND IT: Make your own or buy it at garden centers. If you buy compost, make sure that it doesn't smell sour or like ammonia and that it doesn't contain identifiable plant parts.

Worm castings

Work earthworm castings into the soil before planting or scatter them on the surface after planting. Worm castings are also great in growing mixes for containers and houseplants.

WHAT IT IS: This dark, crumbly, odorless material is the manure of earthworms. It has a nutrient analysis of about 0.5-0.5-0.3.

WHAT IT DOES: Worm castings are a rich source of organic matter. They also contain small amounts of nutrients and are a good all-around soil improver.

HOW TO APPLY IT: Apply 25 pounds (11.25 kg) per 100 square feet (9.3 sq m) to soil low in organic matter. Use 10 pounds (4.5 kg) per 100 square feet (9.3 sq m) if your soil has average fertility; apply 5 pounds (2.25 kg) to the same area of good soil.

WHERE TO FIND IT: Buy worm castings through mail-order catalogs that specialize in organic fertilizers, or produce your own. Buy a commercial worm bin or build your own from untreated lumber. Drill holes in the sides and bottom for aeration and drainage. Keep the bin indoors or, in warm climates, outside in a shady spot. Put pebbles or sand in the bottom and top it with a 4-inch (10 cm) layer of moist bedding. (Make bedding by mixing topsoil and manure with wet peat moss and hay, leaves, shredded newspaper, or dried grass clippings.)

After a few days, add red worms (*Lumbricus rubellus*) or brandling worms (*Eisenia foetida*). Feed them with small amounts of kitchen scraps. Every few months, pull aside the loose bedding and scrape a thin layer of castings from the exposed surface. Add fresh bedding and food to reinvigorate the colony.

Peat moss

Save peat moss for use in potting mixes or as an amendment when planting acid-lovers like blueberries, camellias, mountain laurels, and rhododendrons.

WHAT IT IS: Peat moss is plant debris that has partially decomposed under water, without oxygen, in bogs. Peat is a finite resource because it takes a very long time to form. It has already been depleted in bogs in Ireland and northern Europe, but it is still plentiful in Canada. However, you should use peat sparingly, substituting amendments like compost and shredded leaves whenever possible.

WHAT IT DOES: As a soil amendment, peat moss adds organic matter and increases soil acidity.

HOW TO APPLY IT: Before applying, soak peat moss in warm water to moisten it thoroughly. Spread no more than $2^{1}/_{2}$ pounds (1 kg) per 100 square feet (9.3 sq m). Work the peat moss into the soil rather than leaving it on the surface, where it becomes crusty and sheds water.

WHERE TO FIND IT: Peat moss is commonly sold in bales at garden centers and discount stores. Look for Canadian peat, since Louisiana peat is often of poor quality and excessively acid.

GRASS CLIPPINGS

COW MANURE

If you have excess grass clippings, work them into your garden soil to increase the organic matter content and stimulate soil organisms. Fresh clippings also add nitrogen.

WHAT IT IS: Normally, you should let grass clippings stay on the lawn. But if you've waited too long to mow and the clippings are clumped into piles, rake them up and use them as a mulch or soil amendment. The nutrient analysis of grass clippings averages 0.5-0.2-0.5.

WHAT IT DOES: Worked into the soil, grass clippings add organic matter and stimulate worms and other soil microorganisms.

HOW TO APPLY IT: Work fresh clippings into soil in fall or at least a week before planting. If you have access to large quantities of clippings, you can use 50 pounds (22.5 kg) per 100 square feet (9.3 sq m) for soil low in nitrogen, 30 pounds (13.5 kg) for soil with average fertility, and 20 pounds (9 kg) to maintain good nitrogen levels in fertile soil.

WHERE TO FIND IT: Collect the clippings when you mow the lawn. Because clippings are also an ideal lawn fertilizer, you may want to bag them half the time and let them fall to the ground the other times. If you get clippings from other sources, make sure that the turf they came from was not treated with herbicides or pesticides.

In low-rainfall areas, work cow manure into the soil after harvest. That way, winter rains can leach the high salt content out of the soil before spring planting.

WHAT IT IS: Cow manure, also called cattle or steer manure, is the solid waste of cows and steers. It contains less nitrogen, less organic matter, and more moisture than horse or poultry manure. Its nutrient analysis averages 0.6-0.2-0.5, although this can vary widely. Cow manure is about 17 percent organic matter.

WHAT IT DOES: This balanced fertilizer adds nutrients and organic matter to the soil. Because of its low nitrogen content and high water content, cow manure decays more slowly than horse or poultry manure. In low-rainfall areas, cow manure can raise soil salt content to unacceptable levels.

HOW TO APPLY IT: Add fresh cow manure to the compost pile, or work a 2–4-inch (5–10 cm) layer of fresh manure into the soil in the fall to prepare for spring planting. Use 10–20 pounds (4.5–9 kg) of composted or dehydrated manure per 100 square feet (9.3 sq m) any time of year as a fertilizer or soil conditioner.

WHERE TO FIND IT: Local dairies or feedlots may sell or give away the manure. Be aware that manure from large farms may be sprayed with larvicides to control flies, and it may contain residues of livestock medications. Ask your source about these materials, and avoid manure that you know or suspect might be contaminated. Buy dehydrated manure in bags from any place that sells garden supplies.

HORSE MANURE

Buy dry, bagged horse manure, or haul it from local sources. Commercially available manure is composted to reduce odor, but it's also more expensive.

WHAT IT IS: Horse manure is the solid waste from free-ranging or stabled horses and ponies. When collected from stabled animals, it is often mixed with bedding, such as straw or sawdust. Its nutrient analysis averages 0.7-0.3-0.6, although it can vary widely. Dry manure is easier to work with and transport.

WHAT IT DOES: When worked into the soil, horse manure breaks down quickly, adding nitrogen, phosphorus, and potassium to the soil. It also builds soil organic matter.

HOW TO APPLY IT: Because it is high in nitrogen, horse manure is too strong to apply directly around growing plants. You can spread a 2–4-inch (5–10 cm) layer on the soil in the fall and turn it under, or compost it first. (Composting will also help to destroy any weed seeds that might be in the manure.) Add 10–20 pounds (4.5–9 kg) of composted or dried manure per 100 square feet (9.3 sq m) any time of year.

WHERE TO FIND IT: Local horse owners, riding stables, and race tracks are often glad to supply manure to gardeners, either at no charge or for a small fee. Some manure may contain larvicides or other livestock medications; ask your source about possible contaminants and consider composting the manure before use. Some garden centers sell dried, bagged horse manure.

POULTRY MANURE

Poultry manure is high in nitrogen, especially when fresh. Composted or dehydrated poultry manure is safe to apply to crops any time during the growing season.

WHAT IT IS: Poultry manure is the droppings from chickens, turkeys, and other domesticated birds. Its nutrient analysis averages 1.1-0.8-0.5. It is drier and lighter than cow manure and higher in nitrogen than most manures (except for rabbit droppings). Poultry manure has a strong smell.

WHAT IT DOES: Poultry manure contributes nitrogen, phosphorus, potassium, and organic matter to the soil.

HOW TO APPLY IT: Poultry manure is high enough in nitrogen to "burn" plants; compost it before applying or mix it into the soil. Spread 1 inch (2.5 cm) of fresh poultry manure on the soil in fall, along with an equal layer of high-carbon material like straw or shredded leaves, and work it into the soil. Apply 5–10 pounds (2.25–4.5 kg) of composted manure over 100 square feet (9.3 sq m) any time of year.

WHERE TO FIND IT: Get fresh manure from poultry farms or buy dried manure through garden-supply catalogs. Avoid dusty or old poultry manure, or be sure to wear a respirator if you work around it; it contains fungal spores that can cause respiratory problems.

BLOODMEAL

Bloodmeal is a strong-smelling, powdered fertilizer that is high in nitrogen. It's a great boost for leafy vegetables like spinach, lettuce, and chard.

WHAT IT IS: Bloodmeal (also known as dried blood) is a slaughterhouse by-product. Dried and ground animal blood, sold as a dark, strong-smelling powder, contains about 15 percent nitrogen.

WHAT IT DOES: The nitrogen in bloodmeal is readily available to plants. One application lasts 3–4 months.

HOW TO APPLY IT: If your soil is low in nitrogen, broadcast or side-dress 3 pounds (1.35 kg) of bloodmeal per 100 square feet (9.3 sq m). Lower that rate to 2 pounds (900 g) for soil with moderate nitrogen and 1 pound (450 g) for soil with adequate nitrogen. Keep the bloodmeal a few inches (centimeters) away from plant stems; the high nitrogen content can burn plants. Rake the bloodmeal into the surface of the soil so it will wash into the root zone.

WHERE TO FIND IT: You can buy bloodmeal at garden centers and through garden-supply catalogs; it's one of the most expensive fertilizers.

FISH MEAL

Fish meal is primarily used as a nitrogen source, but it also supplies some phosphorus and potassium. Fish meal has a strong odor and may attract dogs, cats, and rodents.

WHAT IT IS: Fish meal is ground and dried fish parts. Its nutrient analysis averages 5-3-3. Fish emulsion is a similar product in liquid form.

WHAT IT DOES: Fish meal is a general fertilizer that's a good source of nitrogen, phosphorus, and potassium, as well as micronutrients. It lasts one season.

HOW TO APPLY IT: Apply fish meal as a starter fertilizer at planting or as a nitrogen source during the growing season. Broadcast or side-dress at a rate of 3 pounds (1.35 kg) per 100 square feet (9.3 sq m) on poor soil, 2 pounds (900 g) on moderate soil, or 1 pound (450 g) on fertile soil. Apply fish emulsion to leaves or roots according to package directions.

WHERE TO FIND IT: Gardeners that live near an ocean or fish-processing plants have ready access to fish meal. In other areas of the country, it's usually easy to buy fish meal at garden centers or through mail-order catalogs that specialize in organic fertilizers.

ROCK PHOSPHATE

Rock phosphate is an excellent source of phosphorus. For fastest nutrient release, buy the most finely ground material you can find, and rake it into the soil surface.

WHAT IT IS: Rock phosphate is mined from phosphate deposits, washed, and then ground or crushed into a powder. It contains about 32 percent phosphate, although only about a tenth of that is available to plants at any one time. It also is high in calcium and contains a little iron and other trace elements. Colloidal phosphate (also known as soft rock phosphate) is a similar material, with 18–20 percent total phosphate and 23 percent calcium. It is more quickly available to plants.

WHAT IT DOES: Rock phosphate slowly releases phosphorus to the soil. It also raises the pH gradually over time. It is most effective when applied to acid soil (with a pH lower than 6.2) and to soil high in organic matter. One application can last 3–5 years.

HOW TO APPLY IT: Apply rock phosphate directly to the soil in fall, or add it to your compost so microorganisms can make the phosphorus more available. If you apply it to the soil, rake or dig it into the top few inches (centimeters) of soil, so it will be close to the roots. Apply 6 pounds (2.7 kg) per 100 square feet (9.3 sq m) of garden space for soil low in phosphorus. Use 2^1/$_2$ pounds (1 kg) per 100 square feet (9.3 m) for soil with average fertility; use 1 pound (450 g) to maintain good phosphorus levels in productive, fertile soil.

WHERE TO FIND IT: Look in garden centers, farm-supply stores, and gardening catalogs.

BONEMEAL

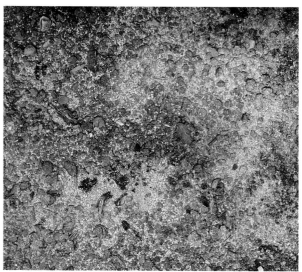

Bonemeal is a popular organic fertilizer for adding phosphorus to the soil. Like rock phosphate, bonemeal is most effective when applied to plants growing in acid soil.

WHAT IT IS: Bonemeal is a slaughterhouse by-product composed of finely ground animal bones that have been steamed. Its nutrient analysis averages 1-11-0, with about 24 percent calcium. Raw bonemeal is slower acting and lasts longer in the soil, but it may be difficult to find.

WHAT IT DOES: Bonemeal adds phosphorus to the soil more quickly than rock phosphate does. The more finely ground the meal is, the quicker the phosphorus becomes available. It lasts for about 6–12 months. The calcium in bonemeal also gradually raises the soil pH. Like rock phosphate, bonemeal is best when applied to plants growing in acid soil.

HOW TO APPLY IT: Apply 3 pounds (1.35 kg) of bonemeal per 100 square feet (9.3 sq m) on soil low in phosphorus. Use 2 pounds (900 g) per 100 square feet (9.3 sq m) on soil with average fertility; use 1 pound (450 g) to maintain phosphorus levels in productive, fertile soil. Rake or dig the bonemeal into the soil to get it close to the roots. If you want to use bonemeal for established ornamental plantings, mix it in with compost and then spread the compost as a mulch.

WHERE TO FIND IT: Bonemeal is commonly sold at garden centers and through garden-supply catalogs. It's almost twice as expensive as rock phosphate.

GREENSAND

Greensand is a slow-release source of potassium. Unlike wood ashes, another common potassium source, greensand does not make the soil more alkaline.

WHAT IT IS: Also called glauconite, this sand-based fertilizer is mined from dried ocean deposits along the northeastern coast of the United States. It contains 6–7 percent potash, along with many trace minerals.

WHAT IT DOES: Greensand is an excellent source of potassium and micronutrients. The potassium becomes available more slowly than the potassium in langbeinite—one application can last up to 10 years. Greensand also contains up to 50 percent silica (sand), so it loosens clay soil.

HOW TO APPLY IT: Broadcast greensand over the soil in the fall. Apply 10 pounds (4.5 kg) per 100 square feet (9.3 sq m) on soil low in potassium. Use 5 pounds (2.25 kg) per 100 square feet on soil with average fertility; use $2^1/_2$ pounds (1 kg) to maintain potassium levels in productive, fertile soil. Greensand is also an excellent addition to the compost pile; the beneficial organisms in the compost help to make the potassium more quickly available to plants.

WHERE TO FIND IT: You can purchase greensand at some garden centers and through mail-order catalogs that specialize in organic fertilizers.

GRANITE MEAL

Granite meal—also known as granite dust—is a finely ground rock. Besides slowly releasing potassium, granite meal is also an excellent source of micronutrients.

WHAT IT IS: This fine rock powder is mined from granite quarries. It contains 3–5 percent potash, along with trace minerals, and 67 percent silica (sand).

WHAT IT DOES: Granite meal slowly releases potassium and micronutrients into the soil solution without raising the soil pH. One application can last for 10 years. Because the potassium is released so slowly, there's no danger of burning plants if you apply too much.

HOW TO APPLY IT: Broadcast 10 pounds (4.5 kg) per 100 square feet (9.3 sq m) to soil low in potassium. Apply 5 pounds (2.25 kg) per 100 square feet (9.3 sq m) to soil with average fertility; use $2^1/_2$ pounds (1 kg) to maintain good potassium levels in productive, fertile soil. Rake it in to incorporate it shallowly; water will wash it deeper into the root zone.

WHERE TO FIND IT: You can buy granite meal at garden centers and through mail-order catalogs that specialize in organic fertilizers.

KELP MEAL

Unlike many other potassium sources, kelp meal breaks down relatively quickly, making its range of nutrients readily available to your plants.

WHAT IT IS: Kelp meal, also known as seaweed meal, is generally made from dried, ground seaweed. Its nutrient analysis averages 1.5-0.5-2.5.

WHAT IT DOES: Kelp meal is a good source of potassium. It also contains calcium, sodium, and sulfur, and it is the best source of trace elements. Kelp meal conditions the soil by adding organic matter and stimulating beneficial soil organisms. Kelp meal and fresh seaweed are both great compost ingredients.

HOW TO APPLY IT: Apply 1–2 pounds (450–900 g) of kelp meal per 100 square feet (9.3 sq m) of garden soil in early spring. Scatter it over the soil surface, or work it in before planting. Kelp meal is very high in micronutrients, so don't add more than the recommended amounts; otherwise the micronutrients could build up to toxic levels.

Fresh seaweed is also a good soil amendment. If possible, rinse to remove the salt before applying the seaweed to your soil. Use it as soon as possible, and dig it into the soil or add it to the compost pile.

WHERE TO FIND IT: Kelp meal is sometimes available at garden centers but is more commonly available through mail-order catalogs that specialize in organic fertilizers. If you live near a shore, you may have access to fresh seaweed.

LANGBEINITE

Langbeinite is high in potassium, and it supplies sulfur and magnesium as well. Because the potassium dissolves easily, it can burn plants if you apply too much.

WHAT IT IS: Langbeinite (also called sulfate of potash-magnesia) is a mined mineral, although some commercial sources are industrial by-products. Its nutrient analysis averages 0-0-22, with 22 percent sulfur and 11 percent magnesium.

WHAT IT DOES: Langbeinite is a source of quick-release potassium. It also adds magnesium and sulfur to the soil without altering the pH.

HOW TO APPLY IT: Broadcast up to 1 pound (450 g) per 100 square feet (9.3 sq m). Avoid using langbeinite if you plan to apply dolomitic limestone to your soil at the same time; otherwise, magnesium could build up to toxic levels. Use another potassium source, like kelp meal, instead.

WHERE TO FIND IT: Look for langbeinite at garden centers or buy it through mail-order catalogs that specialize in organic fertilizers. It is often sold under the brand names Sul-Po-Mag and K-Mag.

WOOD ASHES

GYPSUM

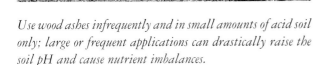

Use wood ashes infrequently and in small amounts of acid soil only; large or frequent applications can drastically raise the soil pH and cause nutrient imbalances.

WHAT IT IS: Wood ashes are the residue from wood fires. Fresh ashes have an average nutrient analysis of 0-1.5-8; leached ashes (those left to sit outdoors) have a lower analysis (0-1.2-2). Wood ashes also contain large amounts of calcium, as well as micronutrients.

WHAT IT DOES: Wood ashes supply potassium; the actual amount varies with the type and age of the wood. The high calcium content raises the pH of the soil.

HOW TO APPLY IT: Apply no more than 2 pounds (900 g) per 100 square feet (9.3 sq m) every 2–3 years because excess amounts can cause nutrient imbalances. Add wood ashes in fall and turn them into the soil in early spring. Since you're applying such a small amount, try mixing them with compost to help get more even coverage. Don't apply wood ashes to acid-loving plants, such as blueberries and azaleas, or around seedlings.

WHERE TO FIND IT: Collect ashes from your fireplace or wood-burning stove, or get them from a neighbor who burns wood.

Gypsum—also called land plaster—supplies the soil with calcium and sulfur. It's especially useful for correcting calcium deficiencies in alkaline soil.

WHAT IT IS: Gypsum is calcium sulfate powder, either mined or produced as a by-product of industrial processes. Mined gypsum is usually gray in color; by-product gypsum is white. Gypsum contains 22 percent calcium and 17 percent sulfur.

WHAT IT DOES: Gypsum adds calcium and sulfur to the soil, generally with little effect on soil pH. It is a particularly effective way to correct calcium deficiency in alkaline soil. Gypsum also loosens tight, clayey soil and helps to neutralize excessive soil sodium and magnesium.

HOW TO APPLY IT: Scatter 4 pounds (1.8 kg) per 100 square feet (9.3 sq m) over soil low in calcium. Apply 2 pounds (900 g) per 100 square feet (9.3 sq m) on soil with average fertility; use $\frac{1}{2}$ pound (225 g) to maintain calcium levels in productive, fertile soil. Don't use gypsum on soil that has a pH below 5.8.

WHERE TO FIND IT: Buy gypsum at garden centers and hardware stores and through garden-supply catalogs.

DEALING WITH PROBLEM SOIL

Gardening would be easier if soil were a more consistent substance. But soil is a complex and changing mixture of powdered rocks and minerals, organic matter, soil organisms, air, and water. And in that mixture there's bound to be something (or a lack of something) that makes gardening a challenge.

Soil problems are usually a package deal. The clay the builders used to cover the backyard of your new house drains poorly *and* has lousy structure *and* is low in organic matter *and* is often too sticky or too hard to work with. Or your rocky soil is too shallow for roots to get a good grip *and* dries out too quickly.

Fortunately, you don't have to solve each problem separately because taking care of one often takes care of the others. Adding organic matter to clay improves the drainage and structure and makes it easier to dig. Building raised beds on rocky soils gives roots enough soil to grow and creates a storehouse for water.

Organic matter is a cure-all for many soil problems, such as soil textures that are too sandy or too clayey. It's a big help with most other problems as well, including excessive alkalinity and compaction. For a few problems, such as severely sloping land or poor drainage caused by a high water table, the solutions often require more of an investment. In some cases, you're wisest to hire someone to do the work or at least to hire a consultant to tell you how to do it.

The main question gardeners with problem soils ask is, "What should I plant here?" This chapter gives a few suggestions; you can get more from garden centers, a local botanical garden, or the county or regional Cooperative Extension Service. When choosing plants adapted to your soil problem—acidity, sandiness, poor drainage, compaction, whatever—make sure they're also suited to the other conditions, such as rainfall, temperature extremes, and amount of light.

"Coping with Slopes" on page 98 covers strategies for gardening on banks and hills, while "Dealing with Poorly Drained Soil" on page 100 offers advice on low, waterlogged sites. If your soil's pH is low or high, see "Gardening in Acid Soil" on page 102 or "Growing in Alkaline Soil" on page 104. In "Handling Saline or Sodic Soil" on page 106, you'll find information on handling these tough sites. If your soil is light and fast-draining, you'll find tips in "Managing Sandy Soil" on page 108; if heavy soil is your problem, look to "Caring for Clayey Soil" on page 110 for answers. "Working with Rocky Soil" on page 112 and "Coping with Compacted Soil" on page 113 can help you handle those troublesome conditions that impede root growth and make digging difficult. And if diseases like club root, crown gall, or root rot are a problem in your garden, see "Dealing with Soilborne Diseases" on page 114 for helpful advice.

No matter what conditions you have, you can find a variety of beautiful and compatible landscape plants. Rugosa rose (*Rosa rugosa*), for instance, is a beautiful shrub that adapts surprisingly well to tough sandy or salty sites.

Coping with Slopes

Slopes and rolling terrain can add interest to your garden, but they also present a landscaping challenge. The biggest problem with slopes is erosion. When it rains, water runs down sloping land. And the soil runs down with it, unless something like plants or mulch covers the soil to stop the impact of falling raindrops and the pace of flowing water. Erosion accounts for why the topsoil on hillsides is thinner than that at the level bottom or top. What's left may be clayey subsoil or gravel and rock; it's often paler because it has less organic matter. And because rain runs off hillsides rather than soaking in, slopes are drier than level land.

How you cope with a slope depends on how steep and how long it is. A long, gentle slope can be easy to manage. A short, steep slope is a little more tricky to handle. A long, steep slope will put you to the test. Whichever one you have, keep one thing in the front of your mind: Even an almost imperceptible slope encourages erosion, so keep the soil covered with mulch or plants as much as possible.

Groundcovers for Gentle Slopes

For a gentle to moderate slope, grass or groundcovers are easy solutions. If you're deciding between the two, consider how difficult mowing a slope is and remember that the grass on the hill will need more water than grass on level ground. If you plan to grow grass and the soil is bare, its often best to lay sod rather than growing grass from seed; otherwise, the seed may wash down the slope before it germinates. If your budget only allows for seed, try covering the slope with biodegradable burlap after sowing.

If you opt for a groundcover, choose a dense one that spreads quickly, requires little maintenance, and is adapted to the soil, amount of light, and your climate. "Plants for Slopes" suggests a few of the best plants for quickly covering sloping sites.

If you're establishing a groundcover on bare soil, mulch heavily with a bulky, long-lasting mulch, such as wood chips

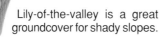
Lily-of-the-valley is a great groundcover for shady slopes.

Slopes with natural or man-made rock outcroppings offer planting pockets for a variety of shrubs and flowers.

or straw, after planting. Or plant a cover crop of oats or millet in late summer; it will die over winter, but the remaining roots and stems will protect the soil from erosion. In spring, you can plant right through the remains and mulch over the dead stems.

Vegetables on Slopes If you grow your vegetables on a sloping site, there are a few tricks you can use to protect the soil from erosion. First, instead of

Spreading shrubs like cherry laurel (*Prunus laurocerasus*) can help to protect the soil on sloping sites.

Planting your vegetable garden so the rows run across the slope will slow water and soil runoff during heavy rains.

planting rows that go up and down the slope, plant rows that go across it. Also, try to avoid stirring up the soil as much as possible. Only dig up the soil right where you'll be planting, and keep all soil well mulched. Living mulches of white clover, as well as cover crops and green manures, are a great way to protect unplanted areas.

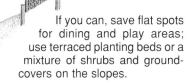

If you can, save flat spots for dining and play areas; use terraced planting beds or a mixture of shrubs and groundcovers on the slopes.

Terraced beds offer attractive, easy-to-plant, level areas for shrubs, flowers, herbs, and vegetables.

Solution for Steep Slopes

For a steeply sloping site, consider building terraces. Terraces are level beds cut into the hillside in a stair-step arrangement. Terraces let you garden on areas that would otherwise erode too rapidly and give you the chance to fill the level beds with better soil than what might be on the slope.

Terraced beds can be made from stone, timbers, or brick—whatever matches your gardening style and your budget. If the walls of the terrace will be less than 3 feet (90 cm) tall, you can probably do the labor yourself; it is definitely worthwhile to consult with a landscape architect beforehand to find out how to make the terraces stable and how to drain them properly. If the walls will be higher than 3 feet (90 cm), let professionals handle the job. Fill finished terraces with a mix of good topsoil and compost, and you're ready to plant.

Dealing with Poorly Drained Soil

Plants need water, but poorly drained soils leave them with too much of a good thing. When the pores between soil particles are filled with water much of the time, plant roots and soil organisms don't get the oxygen they need, so plant and soil health suffers.

Identifying the Cause

An area may have chronically soggy soil for a few reasons. A hardpan—a layer of tightly compacted soil below the surface—may be blocking water from draining. Compacted surface soil can also inhibit drainage. Or the ground may be so low that the water table is not far below the surface. Or the yard may be graded in such a way that water collects in spots rather than draining away.

Handling Hardpans

Hardpans develop naturally in some clay subsoils. Humans can also create hardpans by repeatedly tilling the soil to the same depth. Hardpans are usually between 6 inches (15 cm) and 2 feet (60 cm) below the surface. To check for a hardpan, dig into the soil with a spade or spading fork. If the tool slides in, then stops,

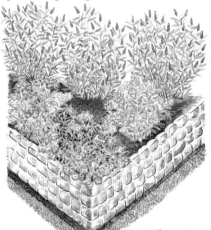

you may have a hardpan. (Or you may have hit a rock— you'll need to dig around a little to see.)

Raised beds increase your planting options on wet sites.

If you have a hardpan and are willing to expend some energy, you can try to break it up. If the hardpan is caused by a clayey subsoil, you may have to repeat your efforts every few years. If the hardpan is human made, you should be able to fix it permanently, provided you don't do what caused it in the first place.

To loosen a hardpan within the top 1 foot (30 cm) or so of soil, use a fork-like device called a U-bar. Use your weight to press the tines into the hardpan, then push the U-bar back and forth. For a slightly deeper hardpan, try double-digging, as explained in "Double-digging for Great Plant Growth" on page 125. If the hardpan is below 2 feet (60 cm) deep, try growing a deep-rooted, water-tolerant legume such as sweet clover to break through the barrier.

Don't settle for ugly, muddy puddles in your yard—brighten them with beautiful plants that appreciate extra moisture.

Building Raised Beds

One solution for poor drainage is to raise the plants above the existing soil. If you're planting trees and shrubs, build low, wide mounds of soil called berms and plant in those. For vegetables and flowers, construct raised beds that are about 6 inches (15 cm) high in cool climates or no more than 4 inches (10 cm) in warm climates (where raised beds can dry out quickly). If you make the beds 3 to 4 feet (90 to 120 cm) wide and leave a walkway between them, you can work the bed from either side without having to step on the soil (which can lead to compaction).

Create temporary raised beds in the vegetable garden by raking soil into broad, flattened mounds. For more permanent beds in any part of the landscape, frame the beds with landscape timbers or wide boards secured

Accent a small wet spot with a clump of moisture-loving plants, like these primroses *(Primula florindae)*.

with braces and anchored with metal stakes. Stone or brick can give beds a particularly attractive appearance for ornamental plantings. Fill the frame with organically enriched soil. When you add soil to build a berm or raised bed, be sure you're not covering the roots of existing trees or shrubs.

Digging a Drain

Soil may also be poorly drained because the water table is high, as it generally is in low areas next to ponds or rivers. Berms and raised beds are fine for small plantings, but if you want better drainage for a large area, you'll need an approach that takes into account the cause of the poor drainage.

If you're determined to have a dry yard, you'll need a drainage ditch or a drainage system of buried pipes to carry away the excess water. Drainage projects of this magnitude aren't a do-it-yourself job; hire a contractor who specializes in drainage systems.

If water collects in spots because the yard is graded improperly, you can have it regraded—another heavy-duty project. You might get around the problem by installing gutters or moving a downspout to reroute some water. Or channel water away from an area by digging a mini-drainage ditch about 8 inches (20 cm)

Astilbes normally perfer shade, but they'll also grow well in sun on a site with steady soil moisture.

deep and just as wide. Fill it with stones so people walking through the garden don't stumble over the ditch and so the mower wheels don't get caught in it.

Picking the Right Plants

Of course, the easiest solution to poor drainage is to look for plants that are naturally adapted to those conditions. A wide variety of trees, shrubs, and perennials can thrive with "wet feet"; see "Plants for Soggy Places" for some suggestions.

Plants for Soggy Places

Try a few of these moisture-loving plants for that wet spot in your landscape.

Trees

Red maple (*Acer rubrum*)

River birch (*Betula nigra*)

American hornbeam (*Carpinus caroliniana*)

Green ash (*Fraxinus pennsylvanica*)

Willows (*Salix* spp.)

Shrubs

Red chokeberry (*Aronia arbutifolia*)

Summersweet (*Clethra alnifolia*)

Red-osier dogwood (*Cornus sericea*)

Winterberry (*Ilex verticillata*)

American elder (*Sambucus canadensis*)

Perennials

Astilbes (*Astilbe* spp.)

Marsh marigold (*Caltha palustris*)

Joe-Pye weed (*Eupatorium purpureum*)

Common rose mallow (*Hibiscus moscheutos*)

Blue flag (*Iris versicolor*)

Yellow flag (*Iris pseudacorus*)

Cardinal flower (*Lobelia cardinalis*)

A wide variety of colorful flowering and foliage plants adapt well to growing along or actually in water.

Gardening in Acid Soil

Of all the problems soil can have, excess acidity is among the easiest to fix. But before you fix it, it's important to find out whether you really need to.

Is It Really Acid?

There are several ways to get a general idea about your soil's pH. Your soil is probably acid if you live in a humid region—the eastern United States or the Pacific Northwest—because rain washes calcium and magnesium (which raise the pH) out of the soil. But there are pockets of high-pH soils scattered throughout these regions, so geography isn't always a reliable clue.

You can suspect your soil is too acid if your plants show deficiency symptoms of nitrogen, phosphorus, potassium, calcium, magnesium, or molybdenum. (For more about these nutrients and their deficiency symptoms, see "Understanding Fertilizers," starting on page 71.) Another clue to look for is acid-tolerant weeds—like plantain, sorrel, and horsetail—growing near your place. Your soil is surely acidic if azaleas, rhododendrons, camellias, and blueberries naturally thrive where you live.

For a more scientific approach, you can test your soil to learn about its pH. For instructions on a simple home test you can do, see "Try a Litmus Test" on page 20. To know for sure how acid the soil is, you have to test it, as explained in "Taking Soil Tests" on page 23.

Lily-of-the-valley adapts well to acidic conditions and produces a thick, weed-suppressing, flowering groundcover.

A slightly acid soil is a great thing to have because most plants thrive in it. But in too-acid soil, most nutrients are bound up in unavailable forms. A few minerals—aluminum, iron, manganese—may become

Adding lime is an easy way to raise the pH of acid soil so you can grow a wider variety of plants in your garden.

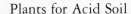

Plants for Acid Soil

Here are just a few plants that appreciate or tolerate soil with a pH below 6.5.

Shrubs

Camellias (*Camellia* spp.)

Heaths (*Erica* spp.)

Mountain laurel (*Kalmia latifolia*)

Bayberries (*Myrica* spp.)

Pieris (*Pieris* spp.)

Azaleas and rhododendrons (*Rhododendron* spp.)

Yews (*Taxus* spp.)

Blueberries (*Vaccinium* spp.)

Flowers

Chrysanthemums (*Chrysanthemum* spp.)

Lily-of-the-valley (*Convallaria majalis*)

Lilies (*Lilium* spp.)

Marigolds (*Tagetes* spp.)

Trees

Firs (*Abies* spp.)

Cedars (*Cedrus* spp.)

Spruces (*Picea* spp.)

Pines (*Pinus* spp.)

Oaks (*Quercus* spp.)

too soluble and reach toxic concentrations. And soil organisms, especially bacteria and actinomycetes, are inhibited, so organic matter breaks down more slowly.

Picking Adapted Plants

Soil with a pH below 6.2 is too acid for many plants, but there are some that will thrive in those conditions. If your soil is naturally quite acid, you may just decide to grow adapted species. "Plants for Acid Soil" offers some suggestions of plants you could try. Observe what is growing well in your neighbors' gardens and in natural areas around your home. Your local botanical garden or Cooperative Extension Service can also recommend plants for your area.

Raising the pH

Add ground limestone to raise the pH, digging or raking it into your soil. Use calcitic limestone, which is almost entirely calcium carbonate, if your soil has enough magnesium. If a soil test shows a magnesium deficiency, use dolomitic limestone, which is magnesium carbonate and calcium carbonate. The more finely ground the limestone, the faster it works; look at the label to make sure that 50 percent of the material will pass through a 100-mesh screen (or at least a 60-mesh screen). Coarser lime may take many years to have a useful effect on pH. Avoid slaked or hydrated lime; these materials can raise pH too quickly, harming roots and soil-dwelling organisms.

As a general rule of thumb, you can raise the pH of 100 square feet (9 sq m) by 0.5 (from 5.5 to 6.0, for example) by adding 2 pounds (1 kg) of lime to a light, sandy soil; 4 pounds (2 kg) to a medium, loamy soil;

Mountain laurel is a late-spring-blooming shrub that is naturally well suited for moist, acid soil and light shade.

and 6 pounds (3 kg) to a heavy, clayey soil. For best results, though, follow the recommendations given on your soil test report. You can apply limestone at any time, but fall is best because it leaves time for the pH to start changing before spring planting. While you're at it, add organic matter, too; the favorable new pH will make microorganisms more active, and they'll be looking for something to eat.

Limestone, a rock powder, can take 2 or 3 years to fully take effect. Three or 4 years after you apply the limestone, test the pH again. If it's still low, make another application. If it's 6.5 or above, you won't need to retest for another 8 to 10 years. Eventually, though, the pH will decrease and you'll need to lime again.

If your soil is very acid, don't try to raise the pH all at once; drastic pH changes can harm plants and soil organisms. Make small applications of lime once or twice a year to change the pH gradually. Ideally, you should take a soil test before each application so you'll know how much material to add or whether the pH is right where you want it. If you routinely add lime without testing, you could raise the pH too much, creating a new set of problems. Repeated applications of dolomitic lime can also lead to excess magnesium in the soil.

Azaleas and rhododendrons thrive in acid soil; a high pH will lead to weak growth and yellowed leaves.

Garden phlox (*Phlox paniculata*) can adapt to alkaline soil, as long as it has good drainage and lots of organic matter.

Growing in Alkaline Soil

In old gardening books, you may find alkaline soils referred to as "sweet soil." Those who garden in alkaline soils, however, find little that's sweet about them. Excessively alkaline soils have chronic nutrient deficiencies and resist attempts to acidify them.

Is It Really Alkaline?

Your soil is probably alkaline if you live in the dry western half of the United States or in one of the small areas with high pH soils in regions that are otherwise acid. Your soil is probably alkaline if your plants have yellow leaves with green veins—the usual symptom of iron deficiency, which is common in alkaline soils. Your soil is definitely alkaline if a mixture of a tablespoon of soil and a tablespoon of vinegar makes a fizzing sound. To get a more definite measurement of the alkalinity, have the soil tested as explained in "Taking Soil Tests" on page 23.

Most plants can live with a slightly alkaline soil. But a soil with a pH above 8.0 starts to take its toll. In too-alkaline soils, phosphorus and most micronutrients are insoluble and unavailable to plants—watch for signs of iron, boron, copper, and zinc deficiencies (as described in "Other Necessary Nutrients" on page 80). On the other hand, minerals like sodium and selenium may be abundant enough to be toxic to plants.

Choosing Compatible Plants

In many cases, you may just decide to grow species that are naturally adapted to high pH soils. "Plants for Alkaline Soil" will give you some ideas of species to start with. Also look around your neighborhood to see what is already growing well there. Ask your local botanical garden or Cooperative Extension Service for recommendations.

Lowering Soil pH

The problem with managing many alkaline soils is that humus and some clays hold huge reserves of the compounds that raise soil pH—magnesium carbonate, sodium carbonate, and calcium carbonate. Those reserves make it hard to significantly lower a high pH: Once you neutralize the alkalinity of the soil solution, the colloids release more pH-raising elements.

The CEC (cation exchange capacity) will give you a clue as to how readily you can lower the pH. (Most soil-testing labs will indicate your soil's CEC on the test report, but it doesn't hurt to ask to make sure you get that information.) If the CEC is between 5 and 20, the soil should respond well. (If it's above 50, the soil is well equipped to resist your efforts; you may just want to grow adapted plants instead.)

The most effective material for lowering the soil pH is elemental sulfur, which is sometimes called flowers of sulfur or garden sulfur. Apply 1 pound (0.5 kg) per

Iron deficiency is a common problem on plants growing in alkaline soil.

Golden-rain tree *(Koelreuteria paniculata)* adapts well to high pH.

Lilacs prefer soil that's slightly acid, but they can grow in alkaline soil, too.

100 square feet (9.3 sq m) for each whole point you want to lower the pH. Rake or dig the sulfur into the soil and keep it moist. Sulfur works relatively fast, and the change can give soil organisms quite a jolt if it's too drastic. If you're applying more than 1 pound (0.5 kg) per 100 square feet (9.3 sq m), split the application and add half in spring and half in fall. A year after you make the final application, retest the soil to see how much the pH has dropped. If the pH is low enough, plan to retest every 3 or 4 years. If it's still above 7.5, make another application.

Organic matter can help lower the pH or keep it low if you've added sulfur. Acidifying mulches and soil amendments include oak leaf mold, sawdust, cypress bark mulch, peat moss, and needles from pines and other evergreens. Besides lowering the pH slightly,

Regular additions of organic matter will help balance soil pH and provide better growing conditions for your plants.

the organic matter will physically and chemically improve the soil, so your plants will be healthier. Avoid fertilizers that raise the soil pH, including wood ashes, bonemeal, rock phosphate, and guano.

If you plan to grow blueberries, azaleas, or another plant that needs extreme acidity, consider growing it in a huge pot sunken into the soil. You can mix your own soil and control its acidity rather than contending with the high pH of the natural soil.

Plants for Alkaline Soil

If your soil's pH is on the high side (7.0 or higher), consider some of these plants; they're naturally adapted to alkaline soil.

Trees

Catalpas (*Catalpa* spp.)
Redbuds (*Cercis* spp.)
Green ash (*Fraxinus pennsylvanica*)
Kentucky coffee tree (*Gymnocladus dioicus*)
Bur oak (*Quercus macrocarpa*)
Black locust (*Robinia pseudoacacia*)
Western soapberry (*Sapindus drummondii*)

Shrubs

Barberries (*Berberis* spp.)
Boxwoods (*Buxus* spp.)
Cotoneasters (*Cotoneaster* spp.)
Forsythias (*Forsythia* spp.)
Chinese holly (*Ilex cornuta*)
Privets (*Ligustrum* spp.)
Pyracantha (*Pyracantha* spp.)
Spireas (*Spiraea* spp.)
Lilacs (*Syringa* spp.)

Flowers

Ageratum (*Ageratum houstonianum*)
Japanese anemone (*Anemone* x *hybrida*)
Snapdragon (*Antirrhinum majus*)
Bergenias (*Bergenia* spp.)
Cosmos (*Cosmos* spp.)
Pinks (*Dianthus* spp.)
Baby's-breath (*Gypsophila paniculata*)
Coral bells (*Heuchera* spp.)
Peonies (*Paeonia* spp.)
Mulleins (*Verbascum* spp.)
Zinnias (*Zinnia* spp.)

Vines

Clematis (*Clematis* spp.)
Virginia creeper (*Parthenocissus quinquefolia*)
Boston ivy (*Parthenocissus tricuspidata*)
Passionflowers (*Passiflora* spp.)

Sea lavender *(Limonium latifolium)* is a tough perennial that is quite adaptable to sites with sandy or salty soil.

Handling Saline or Sodic Soil

You've heard unpretentious people described as being the salt of the earth. Well, with some alkaline soils, the problem is the salt in the earth. If the pH is below 8.5 and the dominant salts contain magnesium and calcium, the soil is saline. If the pH is above 8.5 and the dominant salts contain sodium, the soil is sodic.

Of all the problems a soil can have, being saline or sodic is perhaps the toughest. In saline soils, calcium and magnesium salts pull moisture out of the cells of roots, making them dehydrate. In sodic soils, besides the usual problems associated with high alkalinity, plants must contend with toxic amounts of sodium. And the soil structure is destroyed because sodium makes soil granules fall apart.

The problem begins with abundant reserves of salt in the soil; poor drainage and excessive surface evaporation aggravate the situation. In poorly drained soils, salts in the subsoil can't wash down when it rains or the soil is irrigated. Instead, the water carrying

dissolved salts is drawn upward through the soil, as heat and wind evaporate water from the surface. There, in the case of saline soils, they dry to form a white crust; for this reason, saline soils are sometimes called white alkali. In sodic soils, dispersed humus often percolates to the soil surface, making it black; sodic soils are sometimes called black alkali.

Identifying Salty Soils

How can you tell if salt is a problem? You may have this difficulty in parts of the arid West, along seaboards and gulf coasts, and even in front yards on the winter road-salting route. You may even be able to see the white or black crust on the soil surface.

Choosing Compatible Plants

Even though most plants have trouble coping with salty soil, there are some that can tolerate these tough conditions. "Plants for Salty Soil" will give you some ideas to start with. Also look around to see what is growing well in area gardens and natural areas. Ask your local Cooperative Extension Service or botanical garden for suggestions of plants that are adapted to your particular soil conditions.

Managing Salty Soil

Dealing with salty soil takes a multipart approach. First, make sure that the soil is well drained. If poor drainage is causing the problem, work in ample amounts of organic matter. A drainage system may be the answer for handling large areas. You'll find more suggestions in "Dealing with Poorly Drained Soil" on page 100.

To correct a saline soil, the most effective approach is to dissolve the magnesium and calcium salts and then flush them from the soil, a process called leaching. To be effective, you first have to solve any drainage problems. Without belowground drainage to carry

Coreopsis are easy-care perennials that can take tough conditions, like droughty or salty soil.

away the salty water, it will just percolate back to the surface, bringing more salt with it. Once the drainage is corrected, flood the soil. "Flood" doesn't mean turning on the sprinkler for just a few hours—it means repeatedly drenching the soil. Unfortunately, leaching isn't a viable option in many areas, since locations with salty soil often have limited water supplies. But it can be a help if you're dealing with small sites along salted roads and sidewalks.

If sodic soil is the problem, add gypsum before leaching. Gypsum converts caustic sodium carbonates in the soil to sulfates, which leach more easily. Gypsum also improves soil structure, at least for a couple of years. To apply gypsum, broadcast 5 to 20 pounds (2.5 to 10 kg) per 100 square feet (9.3 sq m), rake it (don't turn it) into the soil, and keep it moist. Go back a week or two later and leach the soil.

Neither installing drainage nor leaching are quick, inexpensive projects. If you have a saline or sodic soil and want to do something right away, mulch the soil to reduce evaporation from the surface. By limiting evaporation, you reduce the amount of salty water entering the root zone. Adding organic matter is also important for helping to improve soil structure.

For new or existing plants, water the soil lightly and frequently to dilute the salt already in the root zone. Don't water deeply or the water will dissolve salts below the root zone, which can then rise to the surface. These waterings are especially important when plants are young and tender. As plants get older and their cells' walls toughen up, they can better tolerate salt.

When you fertilize saline or sodic soils, avoid fertilizers that contain salts, such as langbeinite. And, as you would with any alkaline soil, don't use fertilizers or amendments that raise the soil pH, such as wood ashes or limestone.

Plants for Salty Soil

Soils that have high salt contents call for tough plants. Here are just a few of the plants that are likely to succeed.

Trees

European white birch (*Betula pendula*)

Redbuds (*Cercis* spp.)

Honey locust (*Gleditsia triacanthos*)

Japanese black pine (*Pinus thunbergiana*)

Shrubs

Summersweet (*Clethra* spp.)

Creeping juniper (*Juniperus horizontalis*)

Privets (*Ligustrum* spp.)

Weigela (*Weigela* spp.)

Flowers

Thrift (*Armeria maritima*)

Asters (*Aster* spp.)

Coreopsis (*Coreopsis* spp.)

Pinks (*Dianthus* spp.)

Blanket flowers (*Gaillardia* spp.)

Hostas (*Hosta* spp.)

Statice (*Limonium* spp.)

Oriental poppy (*Papaver orientale*)

Petunia (*Petunia* x *hybrida*)

Phlox (*Phlox* spp.)

Rose moss (*Portulaca grandiflora*)

Sedums (*Sedum* spp.)

Yuccas (*Yucca* spp.)

Plantings along driveways and sidewalks are often exposed to the deicing salts used in cold-winter areas.

Many species of asters are native to seaside areas, so they're naturally tolerant of sandy, salty soil.

Managing Sandy Soil

Sandy soils have a lot going for them, especially when you compare them to clays. They're light to dig in and don't get sticky when wet. They're well aerated. They warm up quickly in the spring. And it's easy to change their pH because they're not buffered by reserves of acidity or alkalinity.

Sands have their flaws, too. They have little clay or humus to hold water and minerals, which wash quickly away between the widely spaced sand particles. With little water in the pores to moderate temperatures, sand gets hot during the day (remember walking across the beach barefoot in the summer?) and cools rapidly at night. The particles may not cling together at all—there's little or no soil structure.

Few soils are pure sands. Most have some silt or clay particles clinging to the larger sand particles, giving the soil a bit more structure and better moisture-holding capacity. Some may even have enough silt and clay to be called a sandy loam, which is pretty close to soil heaven for many plants (especially if you grow root crops such as carrots, parsnips, and turnips).

While it's generally quite easy to tell if your soil is sandy or not, you may want to review the discussion in "Getting a Feel for Texture" on page 16 if you have any doubts.

Regular applications of compost and other forms of organic matter will keep sandy soil in good condition.

Handling the Sand

Compared to other soil quirks, excessive sandiness is pretty easy to remedy—just dump on organic matter. With enough organic matter, sandy soils can hold water and nutrients while still being well drained and easy to work. Of course, with all that extra moisture to heat up, organically enriched sandy soils won't warm up as fast as they normally do in the spring. But they won't get as hot in the summer, either.

Plants for Sandy Soil

Sandy soils tend to be both droughty and infertile. Here are a few plants that can adapt to those conditions.

Trees

Hedge maple (*Acer campestre*)
Gray birch (*Betula populifolia*)
Ginkgo (*Ginkgo biloba*)
American holly (*Ilex opaca*)
Eastern red cedar (*Juniperus virginiana*)
Japanese black pine (*Pinus thunbergiana*)

Shrubs

Japanese barberry (*Berberis thunbergii*)
Summersweet (*Clethra alnifolia*)
Creeping juniper (*Juniperus horizontalis*)
Japanese privet (*Ligustrum japonicum*)
Bayberries (*Myrica* spp.)
Sumacs (*Rhus* spp.)

Flowers

Yarrows (*Achillea* spp.)
Artemisias (*Artemisia* spp.)
Butterfly weed (*Asclepias tuberosa*)
Cornflower (*Centaurea cyanus*)
Snow-in-summer (*Cerastium tomentosum*)
Lance-leaved coreopsis (*Coreopsis lanceolata*)
White gaura (*Gaura lindheimeri*)
Common torch lily (*Kniphofia uvaria*)
Sea lavender (*Limonium latifolium*)
Rose moss (*Portulaca grandiflora*)
Russian sage (*Perovskia atriplicifolia*)
Lavender cotton (*Santolina* spp.)
Sedums (*Sedum* spp.)
Nasturtiums (*Tropaeolum* spp.)
Verbenas (*Verbena* spp.)
Yuccas (*Yucca* spp.)

Sandy soils tend to be dry and infertile, encouraging short, sturdy stems on plants like yarrow.

Because sandy soils are well aerated, microorganisms burn through organic matter quickly. In one way, that's good, because humus forms faster; in another way, that's bad, because nutrient-rich organic matter doesn't last long. Make the best of the situation by adding both fast- and slow-digesting organic matter. Manures, grass clippings, and compost will break down quickly, building humus and improving the soil's ability to hold water and nutrients. Sawdust, wood chips, straw, and other tough materials take longer to break down, providing nutrients for plants and microorganisms and preventing erosion. Growing green manures over the winter is another good source of organic matter. For more information on the different ways you can add organic matter, see "Building Soil Organic Matter," starting on page 41.

While you're waiting for your sandy soil's water-holding capacity to improve, your plants are still going to need water. Because plants use more water when the weather is dry, warm, and sunny than when it's humid, cool, and cloudy, you can't water by a set schedule. Instead, watch your plants—when the leaves look dull or wilt slightly during the heat of the day, it's definitely time to water. Another way to check is to scratch around the top few inches (centimeters) of the soil. Sandy soils are so porous that if the top few inches have dried out, the next few inches below aren't far behind.

Because water infiltrates sand quickly but doesn't hang around long, you can modify the watering rules that apply to tighter soils. Sandy soils can take up water about as fast as you can put it on, so you don't have to worry about water running off before the soil is thoroughly wet. Nor does it take as much water to soak the soil beyond the root zone, which encourages deep roots. But you will have to water more frequently because sands dry out quickly.

Until organic matter in the soil builds up enough to feed the plants, it's a good idea to bypass the soil with foliar feedings of liquid fertilizer. When you foliar feed, plants absorb nutrients through their leaves—you don't have to worry about the nutrients washing past the roots. For more on foliar feeding, see "Applying Liquid Fertilizers" on page 84.

Picking Adapted Plants

Along with, or instead of, improving the soil, you may want to look for plants that are naturally adapted to dry, infertile conditions. "Plants for Sandy Soil" offers some suggestions for plants that might work for you; also consider species that are already growing well in your area. Your local Cooperative Extension Service or botanical garden may have good suggestions for plants that match your conditions.

Sunken growing beds can help to collect moisture around plant roots.

It's hard to beat loose, sandy soil for growing a good crop of great-looking, long-rooted carrots.

With a little work and a lot of compost, you can convert a heavy clay into a loose soil that's ideal for most plants.

Caring for Clayey Soil

If you listen to a group of gardeners talk about their soil, chances are that you'll hear at least a few complaining about clay. They may grumble about it being too wet, too sticky, or too hard to dig; they may gripe about it being difficult to water when dry. It is true that clayey soils can be difficult to cope with, but they aren't impossible to garden in. The trick to handling clay is understanding its characteristics and adjusting your gardening techniques accordingly.

The Characteristics of Clay

Unlike the relatively large, chemically inactive sand grains, tiny clay particles can hold lots of moisture and nutrients. If you work in wet clays, the soil clumps together in clods, which harden when they dry and have to be whacked apart with a hoe or shovel. If clay dries out and bakes in the sun, it becomes as hard as concrete and almost as impervious to water (there's a reason pottery is made from clay). Clays that swell and shrink form gaping cracks when they dry, and they can stick to shovels and shoes when they're wet.

Clays aren't much more fun from a plant's perspective. The tiny clay particles pack tightly together, so water has a tough time draining out from between them. There's little space left for oxygen, unless the clay has dried into a clod, leaving a big air pocket where roots dry out quickly. It's also physically difficult for roots to push through the tight soil.

If you have clayey soil, you probably know it already. If you're in doubt, see "Getting a Feel for Texture" on page 16 to review the difference between various soil compositions.

Loosening Clay Soil

Fortunately, it's fairly easy to improve clays, and when you do, you create a great soil. To loosen up clayey soils, add organic matter. Start by working in a layer of organic matter about 1 inch (2.5 cm) deep in the fall, and see how the soil feels in spring. If the soil is still too clayey, work in another inch (2.5 cm) of well-decomposed organic matter before planting, and check again in the fall. It may take a few seasons to get the soil in the right tilth.

If you want to grow perennial flowers, double-digging the bed will make the soil loose enough for deep roots to penetrate and spread easily. For instructions on this technique, see "Double-digging for Great Plant Growth" on page 125.

Clayey soil holds a lot of water, so make sure the top layer is dry before you irrigate; otherwise, your plants may suffer.

Watering a clay soil requires restraint. Water makes its way into the tiny pores in clay soils slowly. If you apply it too fast, the water that can't infiltrate the soil will run off the surface, taking topsoil with it and running up your water bill. It's better to apply the water slowly, shutting it off every 15 minutes or so to let it soak in. It can take a while to soak the soil past the root zone, but once it's soaked, it stays soaked for several days. Take care not to water too often, or you'll wind up with a water-logged soil that doesn't hold enough oxygen for plant roots or soil organisms.

Improving clayey soil is a viable option for flowers, vegetables, and shrub plantings. But in most cases, you're best off choosing trees that are adapted to your natural soil conditions.

Beyond that, treat clays as you would other soils: Adjust the pH if it's extreme, and use a balanced fertilizer unless a soil test shows that one or more specific nutrients are lacking. It's especially critical to avoid working clay soils when they're too wet; see "When to Work the Soil" on page 118 if you need to refresh your memory on testing soil for readiness. If the soil is too wet, let it sit for a few days and test it again. If the soil is very dry, water it thoroughly, give it a day or two to drain, and then test it before digging.

Picking Adapted Plants

As with just about any soil problem, one management approach is to grow plants that can take your natural conditions. Look for species that are adapted to poorly drained sites and to your soil's particular pH. For some planting suggestions, see "Plants for Soggy Places" on page 101, "Plants for Acid Soil" on page 102, and "Plants for Alkaline Soil" on page 105. Also look to see what is thriving in your neighbors' gardens. Your local Cooperative Extension Service or botanical garden can often suggest other plants that will grow well in your particular soil conditions.

Peonies grow best in loamy, well-drained soil, but they'll adapt to clay if you work in lots of organic matter.

Digging a little sand into a clayey soil won't do much good; you'd need a layer several inches thick to make a difference.

Working with Rocky Soil

To gardeners facing a thin layer of soil over blocks of rock, the usual garden chatter about deep watering and subsoils and double-digging seems rather pointless. In the West and Southwest, some soils are so young that they've barely developed a thin layer of topsoil. In these regions, when you ask a nursery to come plant a tree in your yard, the crew brings jackhammers instead of shovels.

The obstacles these soils present are many. Plant roots have few places to go. Water and nutrients have little to cling to. Tilling, digging, and planting are ridiculously difficult. The usual remedy for building soil—adding ample amounts of organic matter—helps but just isn't fast enough.

Rocky outcroppings usually have pockets of soil that can support plantings of shallow-rooted flowers and shrubs.

Purple rock cress (*Aubrieta deltoidea*) is naturally well suited for rocky, well-drained sites.

What Can You Do?

The best approach to gardening in rocky soil is to use native plants where possible and to import soil for every place else. Plants native to rocky regions have evolved to cope with short supplies of water and nutrients and little room to spread out. They generally have shallow root systems that reach through whatever soil is available.

When working with natives in rocky soil, it's best to begin with the smallest plant possible. Seeds are ideal, although young potted specimens are more practical for trees and difficult-to-germinate plants. Seeds and young plants can grow roots around obstacles in the soil rather than having to adapt an existing root system to new conditions.

Importing soil for raised beds, though expensive, is the only choice if you want vegetables and plants not adapted to rocky soils. (For more details on this technique, see "Building Raised Beds" on page 100.)

If raised beds are too pricey or if you don't have room for them, try growing vegetables and flowers in containers. They'll need frequent (perhaps daily) watering if they're above ground. If you can dig a hole between rocks, you can sink the containers at least partly into the ground so they lose water more slowly. Or try planting in large bottomless plastic nursery containers set on the soil to give roots a little more room to spread in search of nutrients and water.

Rocky soils can't hold much water and dry out quickly, so water them frequently but for short periods. If you choose plants that are naturally adapted to rocky sites, they may not need extra water at all.

If you have large rocks, use them to frame raised beds that will provide more rooting room for your plants.

For More about Natives

For a small fee, you can get lists of native plants adapted to your state through the National Wildflower Research Center. To learn more about the NWRC's information clearinghouse, write to the center at 2600 FM Road 923, Austin, TX 78725.

A clearly marked pathway will help keep people from walking on your flower beds and compacting the soil.

Coping with Compacted Soil

In a unit of "average" soil, about half the space would be soil solids and the other half would be pore space. In a compacted soil, the particles are pressed tightly together, so there is less room for the oxygen plant roots need. Compacted soils are also hard, making it difficult for roots and water to penetrate them. Severely compacted soils support few plants; an exception is prostrate knotweed *(Polygonum aviculare)*, a weed whose presence is a sure sign of compaction.

Heavy clay soils with poor structure become compacted naturally. Compaction also happens to soil that people step, bike, or drive on, or roll wheelbarrows across repeatedly. It's a common problem around newly built homes, where heavy trucks have been driven over or parked on the site.

Plan your garden with plenty of pathways so you don't have to walk or push tools over loosened soil.

Breaking Up Compaction

Once a soil becomes compacted, you need to loosen it up so more oxygen can flow into it. There are several tools you can use to aerate soil. For a small area, you can use a core cultivator, which looks something like a large fork with hollow tubes instead of tines. Press the cultivator into the soil to remove soil plugs; repeat at 4- to 6-inch (10 to 15 cm) intervals over the site. For large areas like lawns, you can rent aerating machines that poke holes in the soil. For more on aerating devices, see the Lawn Aerator entry on page 134.

To loosen up a compacted bed of bare soil, you can occasionally turn it with a spading fork or spade, but be sure the soil is in the right condition to be worked or you'll worsen the compaction. See "When to Work the Soil" on page 118 to learn how to check the soil's readiness before digging in.

Once you aerate the soil, take steps to prevent compaction from happening again. Avoid walking repeatedly over the same area, especially when it's wet. This may mean having to train the kids not to take the shortcut across the yard. If family and visitors continue to walk across the yard instead of on paved paths, consider redesigning the area to make access easier with more formal paths or walkways. Mulching the soil in flower beds and vegetable gardens keeps rain from pummeling and compacting it. Adding compost to clays improves their structure, making them better able to resist compaction.

When planting in a compacted area, loosen the soil well and work a shovelful of compost into the planting hole.

Steady moisture and a soil pH around 5.5 will minimize the chance of scab problems on your root crops.

Dealing with Soilborne Diseases

Much of this book has praised the work that fungi, bacteria, and actinomycetes do in keeping your soil healthy. You've learned how important micro-organisms are for breaking down organic matter, releasing nutrients that plants can use and humus that improves soil structure. But let's face it: When we hear about micro-organisms, especially fungi and bacteria, we usually associate them with diseases. And some of the microorganisms that live in the soil do cause plant diseases. Although these are the minority, they can still have a drastic effect on your crops if they get out of hand.

Common Disease Problems

Some of the most troublesome diseases that can attack your garden plants are caused by pathogens that live in or on your soil. Once these diseases attack, destroy infected plants; then follow the suggestions in "Controlling Disease Problems" to prevent problems in the future.

Fusarium wilt and Verticillium wilt are caused by two common soil fungi that infect a wide variety of plants. They clog up the vascular tissue that transports water from the roots to the leaves and sugars from the leaves to the roots. Affected plants yellow from the bottom up and wilt. If you shave off the side of the stem, you may see dark streaks.

Common scab is caused by an actinomycete. It can affect potatoes, radishes, beets, and other crops, leaving tough, corky blemishes on the roots or tubers.

Crown gall is caused by bacteria and commonly affects brambles and woody ornamentals, like forsythias, euonymus, and roses. Infection causes the stem, especially near the base, to swell and produce a large, tumor-like growth.

Root rot is another disease with a variety of hosts. These fungi can cause roots to blacken and rot while the top growth turns yellow.

Club root is a fungal disease that attacks plants in the cabbage family. The roots become swollen and distorted, and the plants grow less vigorously.

Nematodes are microscopic worm-like creatures that suck the juices out of plant roots, stunting the growth. It's often hard to see specific signs of nematode infestations; the exception is the root-knot nematode, which leaves bumps on the roots.

Club root fungi are less active when the soil pH is 7.2 or higher.

Controlling Disease Problems

Soilborne diseases are among the toughest to control, since they can stay in the soil for many years, waiting to attack any susceptible plants that grow there. The trick is to encourage the beneficial organisms in the soil and to create the best possible growing conditions so plants will be naturally more disease-resistant.

Improving soil drainage or choosing moisture-tolerant plants is an effective way to reduce the chances of root rot.

Use Good Gardening Practices   Follow gardening practices that keep plants vigorous, such as balancing soil fertility and watering at the right time, to help plants fight off diseases.

Grow Resistant Plants   If you know or suspect that pathogens are lingering in your soil, plant disease-resistant or disease-tolerant species and cultivars whenever they are available. This information is generally only available for vegetable crops. The seedling label or seed catalog description will usually tell you what diseases the plant can resist or tolerate.

Mulch   Surround the base of plants with mulch to keep soil that might contain disease organisms from splashing onto plants when it rains. Some mulches actually prevent diseases; for example, composted pine bark mulch prevents some root rots. Compost contains many beneficial micro-organisms as well as compounds that can control some pathogens. When applying any mulch, avoid mounding it around the plant stem; otherwise you may actually encourage root rot. Always leave a mulch-free zone at least several inches (centimeters) wide around the base of the stem.

Adjust Soil pH   Adjusting the pH of your soil can control specific diseases. A soil pH of 5.5 or less will suppress the actinomycete that causes potato scab. The fungal spores that cause club root in cabbage can't germinate in alkaline soils.

Of course, if you're just growing a few potatoes or cabbages, it's probably not worthwhile to adjust your whole garden's pH for these crops. Consider growing them in containers where you can create

Keeping your plants healthy with proper watering and fertilizing is important in preventing disease problems.

the ideal pH and keeping the pH in the rest of the garden near neutral.

Rotate Crops   Rotating crops to different beds each year can break a disease cycle in a vegetable garden. If the host plant isn't present for several years in a row, some pathogens will starve and die out. The beds must be far enough apart that the disease organisms can't move into adjacent crop areas. Plan your crop rotation so that the same plant doesn't grow in the same bed for at least 2 years and preferably 4 or more.

Solarize the Soil   If your garden is plagued with a devastating disease or weed problem year after year, it may be worth the time and effort to solarize the soil. Solarization kills weeds (and any other plants), harmful disease organisms, and most weed seeds, but it generally leaves enough beneficial fungi to repopulate the solarized soil. The main drawback is that solarization takes the affected bed out of production for July and August. And it's not really practical for treating more permanent plantings, like perennial beds, unless you have a nursery bed where you can hold the plants until the treatment is over.

To solarize the soil, first turn the planting area with a garden fork or spade, and smooth it off as if you were preparing to plant. Water the site until it's soggy. The next day, cover the area with clear 3- or 6-mil plastic ("mil" refers to the thickness). Bury the edges of the plastic sheet so that it doesn't blow away or let cool air in. Leave the soil covered for July and August. Once you remove the plastic, the soil is ready for planting. Try not to bring up too much soil by digging or cultivating, or you may bring pathogens up from lower soil layers.

In vegetable gardens, plant crops in different areas each year to prevent buildup of disease-causing organisms.

CULTIVATING THE SOIL

One of the most important steps to growing great-looking plants is preparing the soil well before planting. That means knowing when to work the soil and what tools to use for the task.

For decades, gardeners routinely tilled the soil a few times a year. In the spring and fall, they vigorously and completely turned over the soil in their garden beds, much as farmers plowed their fields. They might later have tilled to work in organic matter, then one more time to control weeds.

Recently, though, the trend in both gardening and farming has been toward less-frequent tilling, and the tilling that does take place is more gentle. The change came about because someone figured out that frequent tilling has some undesirable side effects: It can cause compaction, break down soil structure, throw the populations of soil microorganisms out of balance, and mix organic matter so deeply into the soil that it can't break down readily.

The common practice now is to turn the soil once a year at the most, working in organic matter, fertilizer, and soil amendments at that time. If something needs to be added to the soil during the same year—the second half of a split application of sulfur or potassium, for instance—it's spread on the surface and scratched in with a rake or garden cultivator.

Some gardeners are returning to human-powered tools out of concern about the depletion of fossil fuels and an aversion to noisy, smelly machines. Even if you have a large garden, you can find efficient, easy-to-use, human-powered tools to do the job, such as a wheel hoe with its many attachments.

In this chapter, you'll learn all the tips and tricks you need to know to cultivate your soil properly. "When to Work the Soil" on page 118 will help you decide when your soil is ready for digging or tilling. If you're not sure what soil-working tool is best for you, see "Choosing the Right Tool" on page 120. "Caring for Tools" on page 122 tells how to maintain and store your tools so they'll last a long time. "Digging by Hand" on page 124 covers the basics of turning the soil with your own energy without hurting your back. "Mechanical Tillage" on page 126 offers tips on using and caring for rotary tillers. "Soil-working Tools," starting on page 128, covers 13 different types of tools that you can use in preparing and maintaining your soil. It includes information on when, where, and how to use each tool, along with hints on how to buy and maintain them.

Whether you have a whole collection of garden tools or just a few basic ones, you need to know when and how to use them properly. These skills are an important part of building and maintaining healthy organic soil.

Dig or till cover crops into the soil in early spring, so they'll have several weeks to decompose before you plant.

When to Work the Soil

If you have a truly sandy soil, you can skip this section, because sandy soils drain so fast and are so lacking in soil structure that you can really till anytime (move on to "Choosing the Right Tool" on page 120). But if you have a soil with at least 15 percent clay—that is, if you can form any size "worm" by rubbing a moistened ball of soil between your palms—then when you work the soil is critical.

Protecting Soil Structure

As you learned in "Understanding Soil Structure" on page 18, one of your goals in managing garden soil is developing good soil structure. The soil structure—how the soil particles clump together—goes a long way in deciding how easily plants grow. If the clumps are too big, contact between seed and soil is poor, so germination is poor. Big, hard clumps of soil block expanding roots and create air pockets that can cause roots to dry out. Soil with no clumps at all is a fine powder that becomes hard, compact, and impermeable when it dries after a hard rain. The ideal structure is small, crumb-like granules that hold a good amount of air and water and are easy to dig.

Each time you work the soil, you have a chance to either destroy or maintain good structure. If you dig when it's too wet, the soil forms clods that are hard to break apart once they dry. And walking around on wet soil while you're digging promotes compaction, another factor that can ruin good structure. If you work the soil when it's too dry, the clumps of soil

disintegrate, leaving powder that can blow away in the wind or be carried off by the next rainfall.

Even if you didn't affect structure, there are other good reasons to avoid working very wet and very dry soils. Wet soils stick to everything—your shoes, your tools, and the dog keeping you company. Dry, crusty soils make it hard to push a spade into the ground, so digging is twice as much work as it needs to be.

A Simple Readiness Test

So how can you tell when the soil is at the right stage for digging? Pick up a handful of soil and squeeze it. Then open up your hand. If the soil stays in a firm ball in your palm, it's too wet to work. If it falls apart, it's too dry. If it holds together until you poke it with your finger, it's just right.

Should You Dig in Spring or Fall?

In most cases, your odds of finding soil in just the right condition for digging are better in the fall than in the spring. Rains are usually less frequent in fall, so the soil gets more time to dry out after soakings. If the soil is too dry, you can just water it and wait a day or two.

Fall tilling has other advantages. In the fall, you have several weeks—from harvest until the soil freezes—to fit the garden work into your schedule. In the spring, you only get that fleeting moment between when the snow melts and when it's time to plant. And by working the soil in the

Loose, well-prepared soil provides ideal conditions for great root growth, leading to higher yields.

Waiting until the soil is in the right condition to dig will protect the good soil conditions you've worked to build.

Wait until spring to prepare the soil for annual flowers. Protect the beds over winter with a layer of mulch.

fall, you let it go through a winter of freezing and thawing, which breaks up clods. Then you just have to lightly rake the soil smooth before planting in the spring. If you till manure or another source of organic matter into the soil in the fall, it has time to begin decaying before you plant.

Fall tilling is a bad idea, however, if you garden on a slope because it exposes the loose soil to erosion. Because slopes drain faster than level soils, you may be able to work them in the spring when other soils are still too moist. If you do till in

Digging exposes grubs and other pests to birds.

the fall, cover the soil with a thick layer of straw or another light mulch that you can rake off in the spring. Or protect the soil with a cover crop over the winter (see "Growing Cover Crops and Green Manures" on page 60 for more details).

Cultivation Considerations

So far, this discussion of timing has focused on the big job of turning the soil. But there are other tasks for which you might want to consider the soil's condition. Weeding—whether you hoe or pull—is far easier when the soil is moist (not too wet or dry). So is raking, because clods are more inclined to crumble. And if you're adding solid fertilizer to give plants a boost in midseason, keep in mind that the nutrients will be available more quickly when applied to moist soil. Water very dry soil a few days before you'll be digging, cultivating, or fertilizing. If no rain is expected, watering again after applying dry fertilizer will help to wash it into the root zone.

Good, granular soil is a pleasure to dig and plant in. Careful digging and regular additions of organic matter will help to keep it that way!

Plastic parts are fine for leaf rakes, but you'll need strong metal parts for durable soil-working tools.

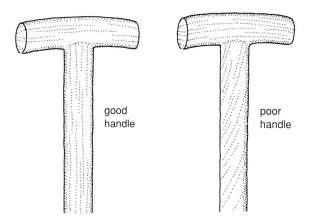

Look for wooden handles that have the grain (the fine lines) running straight up and down; avoid those with angled grain.

Choosing the Right Tool

Using the right tool really does make any job easier, as you know if you've ever used a butter knife when you couldn't find the screwdriver or the heel of a shoe as a substitute for a hammer. But a shopping trip for garden tools can be so baffling that you may well decide to stick with the butter knife and shoe. When faced with a wall-long display of shovels, spades, forks, rakes, trowels, and cultivators, it can be hard to decide what tools, and what version of them, you need.

A Basic Tool Collection

Fortunately, most gardeners can get away with a half-dozen basic tools. You'll need a spade to turn the soil and a shovel for digging holes and for moving soil, sand, and amendments around. A spading fork is useful for turning the soil, working in amendments and green manures, turning compost, and dividing perennials. You'll also need a metal rake for smoothing the soil, a hoe for weeding, and a trowel for planting and transplanting. If you have a huge vegetable garden, you may want to get a rotary tiller, wheel hoe, or even a garden tractor to which you can attach various implements. If you garden in containers, a trowel and hand cultivator will suffice.

Buying Good Tools

There's nothing quite like the feel of working your soil with a good-quality, well-constructed tool. Here are some things to consider as you shop for garden equipment, so you'll get the best tools for your money.

Cost How much you spend for your tools depends on how long you want them to last. If you want to keep the tools for decades, get the best you can afford—$40 for a spade or hoe isn't unreasonable. If you're on a tight budget, if you plan to move in a few years and don't want the extra baggage, or if you leave your tools outside all the time, buy the bargain basement kind for about $15. Be warned, though, that cost-cutting materials and designs make cheap tools more difficult to use than their more expensive counterparts. And cheap tools might not even make it through a season without bending or breaking.

Construction When you go tool shopping, read the label to see whether the metal part of the tool is stamped steel or forged steel. Forged steel is much stronger, but makes the tool cost 20 to 30 percent more than a tubular steel tool. If you want the item to last, go for a forged steel product; if budget is a limitation, consider the stamped steel tool.

Also investigate how the handle attaches to the metal part. Don't buy the tool if the metal wraps only partway around the handle; this construction, called open socket, leaves the wood exposed to water and mud, which can lead to rot. Also avoid tools where the handle is poked onto a spike at the top of the metal portion of the tool, then surrounded with a metal collar to keep the handle from splitting. Neither this type

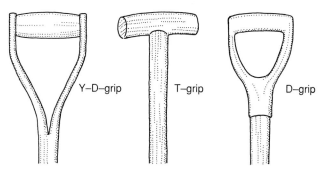

Tool handles come with several types of grips; choose the one that feels most comfortable to you.

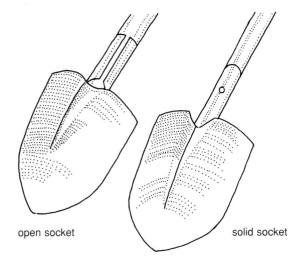

open socket   solid socket

Avoid tools that have the top of the blade partly wrapped around the handle; solid-socket tools are more durable.

of construction, called tang and ferrule, nor open socket is durable and may only last a season or two. Instead, choose tools with metal that wraps all the way around the handle (called solid-socket construction) or has strips of metal bolted to the handle (known as solid-strap construction).

Handles If you want a wooden handle, look for one made of white ash. Handles of spades and forks are sometimes made from hickory, but it's heavier and less flexible. The grain should run the length of the handle, without knots. Painted handles often hide low-quality wood; don't buy them.

Alternatives to wood are fiberglass or solid-core fiberglass. Both are stronger than wood; solid-core fiberglass is nearly unbreakable. Fiberglass adds about $8 to the cost of a tool, while solid-core fiberglass adds about $16. The additional cost is worth it if you want a tool that will last.

Good-quality tools can be expensive, but they are a pleasure to use and can last for many years with good care.

Grips If the end of the handle has a grip for you to hang on to, check how the grip is designed. Make sure it is fastened to the handle and not just slipped over it. Beyond that, the style you choose is a matter of preference (and availability). Try out a few to see which feels best.

Size If you have a choice, pick the handle length that feels most comfortable. Shovels should be at least shoulder height; rakes can be even longer to give you a better reach. A hoe's handle should be long enough to let you stand upright when the blade is about 2 feet (60 cm) from your feet and just about flat on the ground. Short-handled tools, such as spades and spading forks, usually have 28-inch (70 cm) handles, but tall gardeners should look for ones with 32-inch (80 cm) handles. For hand tools such as trowels, choose the length that feels comfortable in your hand. When buying a mattock or pick, choose a weight that you can lift and swing without strain.

If you have a large vegetable garden, a wheel hoe can be an important labor-saving tool for soil preparation.

Take time to put tools away after each use so you can find them later.

Caring for Tools

Once you've gone to the trouble of buying good tools, it's worth a little extra effort to keep them in shape. Without proper care, even the best-built and most-expensive tool can get corroded and dull after a season or two, making it as unpleasant to use as the cheapest department-store tool. When you are ready to dig, you'll be glad of the few minutes you put into keeping your tools clean and sharp.

Keep Them Clean

It's pretty easy at the end of a hot and grimy day in the garden to justify putting the tools away dirty. And you can even get away with it a few times. But eventually the moist soil clinging to your tools will make them rust. And once you finally do get around to cleaning them, the dry soil is harder to get off than the moist soil would have been.

Take time to put tools away after each use so you can find them later.

For that reason, it's a virtue to force yourself into the habit of cleaning your tools when you're done with them. This doesn't mean just scraping the shovel off with the trowel. For one thing, then you have to scrape the trowel off with the shovel, then the shovel off with the trowel again, and so on. Also, all that scraping of metal against metal damages tools.

Better alternatives include using a stick, wooden spoon, or paint stirrer to scrape off the clinging soil. Or use a long-handled scrub brush that you keep in a convenient spot. Another trick is to keep a tub of sharp sand around and dip the tool up and down in it until the soil comes off.

It's especially worthwhile to clean tools before you store them for the winter. Clean off the soil, then use steel wool or a wire brush to remove any rust. Coat the metal with a light oil and hang the tools someplace where you can see and admire them all winter long.

Since your skin touches the handle the most, you may want to keep wooden handles smooth by sanding any rough spots. If you wish, apply varnish or another sealer (like tung oil) to protect the wood. If a handle breaks, pick up a replacement during your next trip to the hardware store; don't just try to tape the old one.

Scrape any clinging soil off the blade of spades, shovels, forks, and hoes to prevent rusting.

Brush your tools off after each use, and give them a thorough cleaning and oiling before storage.

How to Sharpen a Tool

When you sharpen a tool, your goal is to keep the angle of the existing cutting edge but just remove the nicks and thin the edge a bit.

A "mill bastard file" is the file of choice for many tool sharpeners. If you can, find someone to show you how to sharpen, since it's easier to learn from a demonstration than from written instructions. But here are those instructions, just in case.

To begin, hold the hoe where the metal and handle meet, with the cutting edge face down and the handle pointing away from you. Holding the metal file flat against the beveled edge, stroke downward toward the edge of the blade, at a 30 to 40 degree angle to the length of the blade. Use medium pressure and make quick strokes. Go in one direction only—don't saw the file back and forth across the blade. If you find a nick on the hoe's cutting edge, give it a few extra strokes to file it into an edge. Eventually, a small "burr" of metal will form along the opposite edge of the blade. Run the file once or twice along this edge, holding the file flat against the blade, to remove the burr.

To sharpen a spade, turn the tool upside down, so the inside of the blade is facing you. Hold the file at a slight angle, pointing toward the edge of the blade. Push the file from its tip to its handle away from the blade while sweeping the file from one side of the blade to the other. Remove the burr on the opposite side as you would on a hoe, and you're ready to dig.

Keep Them Sharp

Your spade and hoe will do a better job for you if you keep them sharpened. You'll get the best results if you sharpen them briefly and often rather than making it a big job for the end of the year.

For most gardeners, a metal file is an adequate sharpening tool. Use a file that matches the contour of the tool's surface—a flat file for a flat-bladed hoe or spade and a half-round file for a curved shovel blade. If you have many tools, a whetstone or grindstone will take care of them more quickly. For more tips on sharpening your own tools, see "How to Sharpen a Tool." If you don't want to sharpen them yourself, you can take your tools to someone who does it professionally. The best time to do this is in late fall, as you are preparing your tools for storage. Sharpeners are often swamped with work in spring, and they may not have time to do your tools as soon as you need them if you wait until the last minute.

Maintaining a Tiller

If you own a rotary tiller, you'll need to clean off the soil after each use. Wash both the tines and the body with a soft cloth. If you keep the painted parts waxed, the soil will come off more easily.

Look for any loose or missing screws, nuts, or bolts; replace as necessary. Once a year, or every 25 hours of use (whichever comes first), clean the air cleaner by tapping it against something; if it's really filthy, wash it. You'll need to clean it more often if your soils are powdery. Use the same timetable for changing the oil. Change the spark plug every year, too, or every 50 hours of use.

Before storing the machine for winter, clean out the fuel line by draining out all the gasoline and then running the machine until it stops. Remove, clean, and replace the spark plug, leaving the spark plug wire disconnected. If the machine has a four-cycle engine, change the oil. Check the blades or tines, and sharpen them if needed. See your owner's manual for other suggested maintenance steps.

For years of dependable service, keep your tiller clean.

Digging by Hand

There's nothing quite like the feel of working your soil with your own power. It's really rewarding to sink a spade deep into a garden bed and turn over a rich, dark, crumbly mass alive with earthworms and other soil creatures. Hand digging is certainly good exercise (if you do it properly!), and it doesn't contribute noise and pollution to the environment. It is also less destructive to the soil structure and soil organisms than power tilling.

There are several tools that move earth well, each in a different way. Spades have short, flat blades that are useful for cutting sod, digging holes, and turning soil. Their waist-high handles make it easier to toss dirt aside. Shovels are good for moving sand or soil around. Some gardeners like to use them for digging instead of a spade. For tall people especially, a shovel's longer handle often makes it easier to dig with than a spade. Trowels are perfect for making small holes for transplants and bulbs and for other down-on-your-knees digging chores.

Spading forks do many of the things spades do, only with less effort. They're great for turning green manures and other organic matter under the soil and for harvesting root crops. You can also use them to turn compost piles and aerate the soil. Rakes are useful for making the surface soil level and smooth. You can use both the side with tines and the flat back.

To learn more about the use and care of each of these tools, see "Soil-working Tools," starting on page 128. For specific tips on safe digging, see "Spare Your Back."

Loose, well-dug soil is vital for great harvests from potatoes, carrots, and other root crops.

Double-digging for Great Plant Growth

Digging the top 8 inches (20 cm) or so of your soil will provide good growing conditions for most annual plants. But in many cases, digging twice as deep can give you twice the benefits. Double-digging is a useful technique for breaking up compacted soil below the surface, improving drainage. It also provides twice the rooting room for deeper-rooted plants, like perennials. There's no doubt about it—double-digging is a lot of work. Fortunately, the beneficial effects can last for years. And the strong, vigorous growth of your plants will more than repay the few hours of sweat you invested before planting.

Warming Up

The soil is ready, you've got the right tools, and you're eager to dig in. To be sure your rush of enthusiasm doesn't leave you groaning all night, follow these tips for preventing post-digging back anguish.

First, warm up by gently stretching your back, legs, and arms. Then briefly do something to get the blood flowing—swing your arms from side to side, walk around briskly, jog in place.

stretch legs

stretch back

swing arms

jog in place

If Monday mornings often find you aching from a weekend of digging, don't give up on the garden; learn how to dig the right way! Here are some tips that can help save your muscles next time you turn the soil.

First, insert the tool into the soil so the blade is straight up and down. Now follow these steps:

1. Keeping your back straight and your foot on the upper edge of the spade, use your weight to push the spade into the soil.

2. Bend both your waist and knees as you slide the spade under the soil, then straighten both to lift the load.

3. Turn your whole body before depositing the dirt—don't just twist your torso as you fling the soil off to the side.

It's easy, in your rush to finish up, to ignore pain. But pain has a purpose, and that purpose is to tell you to knock it off and go in the house for some lemonade. You'll get more done and feel better if you take regular breaks, preferably before you start to feel pain!

Before digging, make sure the soil is at the right moisture level, or you may end up doing more harm than good; see "A Simple Readiness Test" on page 118 for details. If the soil is too dry, soak the area and then wait a few days before digging. If you are preparing a new area, strip off the sod before double-digging.

Start at one edge of the area by digging a 1-foot (30 cm) wide, 8- to 12-inch (20 to 30 cm) deep trench. Put the soil you are digging in a wheelbarrow. Spread a 1- to 2-inch (2.5 to 5 cm) layer of finely textured organic matter such as compost or aged manure over the newly exposed soil in the trench, and add any fertilizers or amendments the soil needs—perhaps lime or sulfur to adjust the pH, or maybe a source of phosphorus. Use a spading fork to loosen the subsoil by sticking the tines through the amendments and wiggling them around in the soil.

Then step backward to dig the second trench. Slide the soil from this 1-foot (30 cm) strip into the first trench, then work organic matter and amendments into the newly exposed bottom layer of soil. Repeat the process of moving a top layer and loosening the bottom layer until you get to the last strip. Cover the last bottom layer with the soil in the wheelbarrow.

All that loosening and amending will raise the soil level a few inches (centimeters). Give it a few weeks to settle before you plant. Never walk directly on the loosened soil, or you'll undo all your hard work. If you must step into the bed, lay broad boards over the bed, and walk on those instead; lift the boards when you're done.

Spading forks are useful for harvesting root crops and for digging green manure crops into the soil.

Annual and perennial flowers will thrive in well-prepared soil.

The rapidly spinning tines of rotary tillers make short work of preparing your garden soil for planting.

Mechanical Tillage

Rotary tillers are gasoline-powered devices that make tilling the soil far faster and easier than hand digging. They have disks with metal tines, mounted on a central axis. When the axis spins, the tines whip through the soil, breaking it up. These machines can make short work of breaking new ground, working in organic matter, aerating compacted topsoil, and digging under green manures.

The Trouble with Tillers

Their speed and power make rotary tillers very useful, but they do have several drawbacks. For one thing, they're a big investment. Unless you have a huge garden, you may not want to spend the money for a machine that you'll only use for a few hours each season. (Of course, if you can't afford to buy your own tiller, you can usually rent one for a day or weekend for a reasonable fee.) Tillers also use gasoline, which bothers gardeners trying to cut back on the use of fossil fuels. And some people just don't like the noise.

But perhaps the biggest drawback is that they are tempting to use, and their overuse can damage the soil. The spinning metal blades can break crumbly granular soil into fine powder, ruining soil structure. If you repeatedly till to the same depth, you can create a layer of hardpan right below the blade depth. Finally, tillers work in large quantities of air, which can cause a population boom of

Rear-tine tillers are expensive but powerful.

soil microorganisms. While this is good to some extent, the stimulated microorganisms can rapidly deplete your soil's supply of organic matter unless you add enough material to make up for it.

Getting the Right Tiller for You

There are two basic types of tillers on the market. One has the tines mounted in front of the engine, and the other has the tines behind the engine. If you're shopping for a tiller, take into consideration how big an area you need to till, how much money you are prepared to spend, whether you'll need to transport the machine elsewhere with any regularity, and how strong you are.

A rotary tiller with the tines behind the engine is the best investment if you're tilling a lot of land because it will propel itself through the soil in a fairly straight line, making your job easier. But these rear-mounted tillers are quite expensive, as well as big and heavy—not the sort of thing you can toss into the trunk when a friend wants to use it.

Rotary tillers with the tines in front of the engine are far cheaper, lighter, and easier to turn in small places. But they're not self-propelled—you have to

Tillers are particularly useful for large gardens where the entire area is cultivated each year.

shove them forward, which makes them more tiring to use. They're harder to control and can run away if you're not strong enough to guide them.

Since tillers became popular, dozens of styles of all different weights and sizes have found their way to market. Before you invest in one, try out several. Or skip the investment by renting them; just make your reservations early— tillers are a popular item at rental centers during the spring planting season.

Tips for Trouble-free Tilling

As with digging, only till when the soil is damp but not wet, and try for fall rather than spring tilling. Tillers are so powerful that it's easy to convince yourself they're invincible. They're not, so don't get your machine into situations it's not designed to handle, such as rocky soil or soil covered with tough plant residues. Don't expect it to do every job in one pass; you might have to make a few passes to loosen a compacted soil or work in a green manure.

Don't use a mechanical tiller to remove sod where you want to put a garden or flower bed. First of all, grass roots may be too thick and tough for most tillers. Strong tiller blades will chop the grass rhizomes into minute pieces, all of which have the potential of sending up a new grass plant where you no longer want one. The same caution applies to sites with spreading perennial weeds like Canada thistle, quack grass, and bindweed; if you don't remove the weeds before tilling, you could create a nightmare of new weeds popping up in your new garden. For severely weed-infested areas, it's worth taking the time to carefully dig out the roots of these tough pests by hand before tilling or planting.

Don't till areas where Canada thistle grows; each piece of root can produce a new shoot.

Wait until the soil has dried out in spring before you till; working wet soil causes compaction, which inhibits root growth.

Work in extra organic matter every time you till to maintain healthy soil for healthy crops.

SPADES

For extra strength, look for a spade with a forged-steel blade instead of a stamped-steel blade; the label should tell you. The handle grip should be comfortable and firmly attached.

WHERE AND WHEN TO USE: Use a spade to turn soil, remove sod, or cut straight edges between lawns and beds. The square edge and flat blade also make spades handy for digging trenches.

HOW TO USE: To push the blade into the soil, rest your foot on the top rim of the blade and lean your body weight onto it. Pull the handle back and down. When lifting, bend your knees and slide one hand down the handle; if possible, brace the handle of the spade with your thigh.

HOW TO BUY: For many gardeners, a spade is one of the most used gardening tools, so it's worthwhile to invest in a top-quality one. Some gardeners indulge in a stainless-steel blade, although heat-treated or epoxy-coated blades are almost as easy to use and last a long time; they're cheaper, too. Some blades have the upper edge (the place you put your foot) bent over to form a tread; this makes the tool somewhat more comfortable to use and keeps the blade from cutting your leg if your foot slips off.

The standard spade handle is 28 inches (70 cm). If you're tall (over 6 feet [1.8 m]), a 32-inch (80 cm) handle may be more comfortable. See "Buying Good Tools" on page 120 for more buying tips.

HOW TO MAINTAIN: Sharpen lightly when the blade is too dull to cut well. Brush off any clinging soil after each use. At the end of the season, scrape off any rust with steel wool or a metal brush and rub the blade with a light coating of oil.

SHOVELS

Shovels are handy for digging holes or for scooping up loose materials. For good leverage, the handle should reach your shoulder at least; your nose is even better.

WHERE AND WHEN TO USE: Shovels are most commonly used for moving loose material such as sand, soil, or soil amendments. Many gardeners also use them for digging.

HOW TO USE: When digging with a shovel, use your foot to push the blade into the soil. Use your legs and arms, not your back, to lift the load. Before tossing the load, turn your whole body, not just your upper torso, in the direction of the toss.

HOW TO BUY: Look for a forged-steel blade, which is stronger than one made of stamped steel. Ash handles are strong; fiberglass handles are stronger. Shovels vary in the width and depth of the scooping blade. Choose the one that you can work with most comfortably when the scoop is full.

HOW TO MAINTAIN: After using, scrape off all clinging soil. Sharpen as needed to keep the edge in good cutting condition. Before storing the shovel for the winter, remove any rust from the scoop with a steel wool pad or wire brush, then coat the metal lightly with oil.

FORKS

Forks may have rectangular or square tines; rectangular (flat) tines are best for digging. The tines on pitchforks are longer and more flexible than those on other forks.

WHERE AND WHEN TO USE: Spading forks and English garden forks are useful in many areas of the garden. Use them for turning heavy or rocky earth, working cover crops and organic matter into the soil, fluffing compost, aerating soil, lifting root crops, and dividing clumps of crowded perennials. A border fork is a smaller version of the spading fork. Pitchforks are for fluffing compost and moving piles of hay or straw, but not for digging.

HOW TO USE: To turn soil or work in organic matter, use your foot to push the tines into the soil, lift the fork, then dump the load with a twist of your arms and wrists. Avoid using a fork to pry rocks out of the soil or you'll bend the tines.

To fluff compost, dig the tines into the compost at a 45 degree angle and lift it with a slight toss. To aerate a lawn, use your foot to push the fork into the soil, then push the handle back and forth. Separate perennial clumps by inserting the fork to loosen the center, then pull the crown apart with your hands; or use two forks inserted back to back and push them away from each other.

HOW TO BUY: For top quality, get forged rather than stamped steel for the fork and white ash or fiberglass for the handle.

HOW TO MAINTAIN: Remove clinging soil after each use. At the end of the season, scrape rust off with steel wool or a wire brush and wipe with oil.

BROADFORKS

![broadfork image]

Use a broadfork to prepare raised or previously worked beds for planting, to aerate compacted soil, and to break up a hardpan. Work the soil when it's slightly moist.

WHERE AND WHEN TO USE: Also called U-bars or bio-forks, broadforks are used to deeply loosen soil without turning it like forks and spades. Broadforks don't loosen or aerate the soil as much as double-digging does. They're good tools to use if you don't want to mix poor-quality lower soil layers with the topsoil. Broadforks are also useful for beds with fragile soil structure, heavy soil that needs frequent loosening, or sandy soil that you don't want to over-aerate.

HOW TO USE: Rest your foot on the crossbar that the tines are attached to. Use your body weight to push the tines into the soil. If you're loosening the soil for planting, pull the handles toward you and push down so the tines lift out of the soil. To break up a hardpan, push the tines into the soil, then push and pull the handles back and forth.

HOW TO BUY: Broadforks vary in weight and size; find one that's tough enough to do the job but easy to manage. Heavy ones often have two handles that rise vertically from the crossbar that hold the tines. Lighter ones often have a handle that's topped with a horizontal crossbar, which is more comfortable to grip.

HOW TO MAINTAIN: Remove all clinging soil from the tines. At the end of the season, scrape any rust off all metal parts with steel wool or a wire brush, then coat the metal with light oil.

MATTOCKS

A mattock is a handy tool to have when you're wrestling with hard, rocky soil or digging out stubborn stumps. Choose a mattock with a durable hardwood handle.

WHERE AND WHEN TO USE: Mattocks, also called grub hoes, are handy for removing stumps and breaking up hard or rocky soil that gets in the way of your landscaping plans. You can also use them to dig holes.

HOW TO USE: Use a swinging motion with the pick end to sever woody plant roots and to break up stony soil. Use the blade with a chopping motion for digging a hole or for prying rocks you've loosened with the other end.

HOW TO BUY: Mattocks have a pick at one end and a hoe-like blade at the other. The metal part should fit snugly into the opening in the handle; it shouldn't twist when you push and pull on it. Mattocks vary in weight. Heavy ones are best for digging in very hard or rocky soil; regular mattocks are fine for normal use. You should be able to swing the tool comfortably.

HOW TO MAINTAIN: Remove clinging soil after use and rub with an oily rag to prevent rust. Sharpen the blade end when it becomes dull.

CROWBARS

Keep a crowbar for tackling tough garden chores, like prying out rocks or digging out stumps. The heavier the bar, the more it can lift without bending.

WHERE AND WHEN TO USE: A crowbar—also known as a caliche bar, pry bar, or axle rod—is a handy tool for prying large rocks, stumps, or pieces of broken concrete out of the ground. You can also use it to break up tight caliche soil (found in the Southwest), make holes in hard soil for garden stakes, or roll big rocks into place when building a stone wall.

HOW TO USE: When prying out a rock, use the edge of the hole or another rock as a fulcrum: Put the bar's tip under the heavy rock, rest the center of the bar on the fulcrum, and push down on the free end.

HOW TO BUY: A true crowbar is a 4–5-foot (1.2–1.5 m) long, skinny, straight steel bar. The end is either pointed or angular. Look for a bar made of high-carbon steel.

HOW TO MAINTAIN: Clean off clinging soil after use.

TROWELS

A trowel is one of those basic tools that no gardener should be without. Look for trowels that are all cast aluminum or that have metal scoops and wooden handles.

WHERE AND WHEN TO USE: Trowels are standard equipment for on-your-knees digging. Use a trowel when digging a hole for bulbs or transplants, making a furrow for seeds, or even weeding around small plants. Transplant trowels have particularly narrow, cupped blades that are handy for planting or working in small spaces.

HOW TO USE: Dig holes by using the trowel as a scoop to loosen and lift the soil. Or hold the handle in your fist with the face of the blade pointing toward you, and dig by stabbing the soil and pulling back and up.

HOW TO BUY: The blades come in different widths and lengths, with shallow to deep scoops. Avoid cheap trowels that are pressed out of a single sheet of metal; they are no bargain. Make sure the handle and weight feel comfortable to you; one with a plastic cover might prevent blisters. Plastic handle covers on one-piece aluminum trowels can also keep your hands from turning black.

HOW TO MAINTAIN: Clean off clinging soil after use. At the end of the season, clean thoroughly and dry, then coat the metal with oil before storing. It's easy to lose a trowel in the garden, so wrap a strip of bright tape on the handle to help you spot it.

RAKES

For easiest raking, the tool's handle should be as tall as your nose, and its head should be heavy enough to remain on the soil as you push it around.

WHERE AND WHEN TO USE: A metal garden rake is an indispensable part of any garden tool collection. Use rakes for clearing stones, leaves, sticks, and other debris from beds and making a smooth surface for planting. Rakes are also handy for forming and shaping raised beds, working fertilizer into the soil, and spreading manure, compost, mulches, and other organic matter across the soil surface. If you're smoothing the soil before planting, work when the soil is slightly moist.

HOW TO USE: Both the tines and the back of the rake are useful for pushing and pulling soil and organic matter around.

HOW TO BUY: You can choose between two basic types of rakes: straight head and bow. The metal bar the teeth are attached to is straight in the straight head, curved in the bow. The bow gives more spring and clings to the ground better. Rakes vary in width; the wide ones are hard to maneuver in small places. Choose a rake made with forged rather than stamped steel and with a hardwood or fiberglass handle.

HOW TO MAINTAIN: Clean debris from between the tines after using, and scrape off clinging soil. Scrape off any rust with steel wool or a wire brush at the end of the season, and coat the metal lightly with oil.

LAWN AERATORS

Lawn aerators may have spikes to punch holes in the soil, or scoops or hollow tubes to pull out plugs of grass and soil; the plug-removing kinds are more effective.

WHERE AND WHEN TO USE: A lawn aerator is used to loosen compacted soil in lawns and gardens. It lets air, water, and nutrients reach the root zone where they are needed. Aerate compacted areas every 2–3 years, in spring or fall.

HOW TO USE: Spike aerators open small channels in the soil, but they also can cause compaction in the soil around the holes. The preferred tool—usually called a core aerator—is the kind that pulls out plugs. Use a manual core aerator, poking it into the soil at 4–6-inch (10–15 cm) intervals, or rent a power core aerator. Leave the cores on the surface, or rake them up and add them to the compost pile.

HOW TO BUY: For small- to medium-sized yards, rent a core aerator or buy a hand-held or walk-behind (motorless) aerator. You can also buy lawn aerator sandals, which are basically spiked platforms you strap on the bottom of your shoes; wear them when you're walking around your yard. For large lawns, renting a core aerator every few years is the best way to go.

HOW TO MAINTAIN: If you buy an aerating device, clean it after each use. Remove any soil that gets stuck in the openings of a core cultivator.

CULTIVATORS

You can choose from a variety of different types of cultivators for uprooting young weeds, aerating the soil, and scratching in dry fertilizers.

Any kind of cultivating is usually easiest when the soil is slightly moist. If conditions aren't ideal, it's better to work with soil that is too dry rather than too wet.

WHERE AND WHEN TO USE: Depending on the type of cultivator, you can use it to loosen and aerate the soil, scratch in dry fertilizer, and pull out weeds. Hand-held cultivating tools are good for working around the base of plants and other small spaces.

HOW TO USE: The exact method depends on the type of cultivator.

ASIAN HAND CULTIVATORS: These resemble a trowel with a pointed end. The blade curves into a scooped shape, making it useful for deep cultivating.

CAPE COD WEEDERS: This tool has an L-shaped blade; pull the blade along just below the surface for weeding and loosening the soil.

DANDELION WEEDERS: Also called asparagus knives or fishtail weeders, these tools have a blade that resembles a forked tongue; use them to dig out weeds with long taproots and to harvest asparagus.

HAND CULTIVATORS: These handy tools have three claw-like tines and either a short or long handle. Use them to work closely around plantings, rake weeds from the soil, or scratch in a side-dressing of dry fertilizer. Spring-toothed weeders are similar, but a spring gives the tines some bounce, making them more flexible.

HAND FORKS: Hand forks resemble small garden forks and can work the top 4 inches (10 cm) of soil or make holes for transplants. They're good for tight places.

HEART HOES: Also called one-prong cultivators, these have a single C-shaped tine with a heart-shaped end. They let you work close to plants without doing damage. (A long-handled version may be called a biocultivator.)

HOTBED WEEDERS: Hotbed weeders have a C-shaped blade that cuts along three of its edges, making them good for cutting small weeds in tight places.

PAVEMENT WEEDERS: These have an angled, pointed blade that you scrape between sections of sidewalk or driveway. (An old kitchen knife will work just as well.)

HOW TO BUY: When choosing a hand-held cultivator, make sure it feels comfortable. If you do a lot of work close to plants, buy a tool with a small blade that's easy to control.

HOW TO MAINTAIN: Clean after each use. At the end of the season, use steel wool or a wire brush to remove any rust, then cover the metal with a coating of oil. These small tools are easy to misplace. If yours doesn't have a colored plastic handle, wrap a strip of bright tape around the handle to help you spot it on the ground.

HOES

Hoes are handy for a variety of garden tasks—creating hills and raised beds, laying out rows, digging furrows, and weeding and cultivating around plants.

When buying a hoe, look for one with a beveled, rather than flat, blade. Keeping a good edge on your hoe with regular sharpening will make weeding much easier.

WHERE AND WHEN TO USE: Hoes are generally used for slicing weeds off at soil level. The eye hoe, an exception, is designed for heavy digging and moving soil. Hoeing is easiest when the soil is slightly moist.

HOW TO USE: If you're using a standard pull or draw hoe—where the neck of the hoe curls back toward you—position your hands with your thumbs pointing up and pull the hoe toward you with a sweeping motion. If you use a push hoe—with the blade pointing away from you—hold the handle with your thumbs pointing down. Push it in front of you as you walk, with the blade just under the soil surface.

HOW TO BUY: Choose a hoe with a white ash or fiberglass handle, joined to the metal with solid-socket or solid-strap construction. Beyond that, look for a hoe that suits your needs and taste.

AMERICAN PATTERN HOES: These are the ones that come to mind when most people think of hoes. The blade is broad and straight, measuring about 6 inches (15 cm) across and 4 inches (10 cm) deep. They don't require much bending over to use.

EYE HOES: Eye hoes have sturdy, heavy, deep blades. They are used for breaking ground, making terraces, and digging.

ONION HOES: Onion hoes are similar to American pattern hoes, but the blade is wider across and less deep—about 7 inches (17.5 cm) by $1^{1}/_{2}$ inches (3.7 cm). They are good for cutting weeds below the soil surface.

OSCILLATING HOES: Also called hula or action hoes, these have a loop of metal fastened to the handle with a hinge. This blade wiggles back and forth, cutting weeds with both the push and the pull stroke. Because it hardly disturbs the soil, it doesn't bring dormant weed seeds to the surface.

SCUFFLE HOES: These are generally sharpened on the front edge to cut on the push stroke.

SWAN-NECK HOES: These tools have a long, curved shank or neck that lets the blade sit almost flat on the ground. They're good for doing light weeding without having to stoop.

WARREN HOES: These have an arrow-shaped blade and are good for gouging out clumps of weeds.

HOW TO MAINTAIN: Remove all clinging soil after each use. Coat the metal with oil before storing for the winter. Sharpen the blade often with a flat metal file to make cutting easier.

WHEEL HOES

ROTARY TILLERS

Wheel hoes are most useful in large vegetable gardens with long, straight rows. You can buy these tools with attachments for seeding, hilling, raking, and other tasks.

WHERE AND WHEN TO USE: Wheel hoes are most useful in large vegetable gardens. Depending on the attachments you get, you can cut off weeds growing between rows of crops, work fertilizer and soil amendments into the top layer of soil, break ground for a new garden, and take care of many other garden tasks. The soil should be slightly moist when you work it.

HOW TO USE: To move the wheel hoe forward, push with quick, short thrusts, or rock it from side to side slightly to wiggle it forward through the soil. Bend your arms at the elbows. Keep the blade flat and just below the surface of the soil.

HOW TO BUY: Look for a wheel hoe that has the attachments you need. You can buy one with a large wheel—about 22 inches (55 cm) in diameter—or a small one, with a wheel about 12 inches (30 cm) in diameter. Some gardeners feel the larger wheel is easier to push; others feel the smaller wheel is more stable and powerful. Some wheel hoes can be adjusted to the user's height.

HOW TO MAINTAIN: Clean after each use. At the end of the season, scrub off any rust with steel wool or a wire brush, and coat the metal with oil.

Rotary tillers are a big investment; you'll pay a few hundred dollars for a front-tine model, about a thousand for a rear-tine model. Do some research before you buy.

WHERE AND WHEN TO USE: Use a rotary tiller for preparing bare soil for planting and for working in amendments or green manure crops. Tillers are most useful in medium to large vegetable gardens or annual flower beds. Avoid using rotary tillers to clear a sodded area: They can cause weed problems by chopping up the plants and perennial weed roots and spreading them through the soil. Till the soil only when a soil ball, made in your fist, easily falls apart when touched. Tilling when the soil is too wet or too dry can destroy soil structure.

HOW TO USE: Exactly how you'll use your tiller depends on its construction. Read the owner's manual for specific instructions. If you plan to till under a green manure or cover crop that's more than a few inches (centimeters) tall, mow the crop first and let it dry for a day or two.

HOW TO BUY: Decide whether you need a big, expensive, rear-tine tiller or if you can make do with a smaller, cheaper, front-tine one that is less powerful. Ask around, read consumer magazines, and rent or borrow as many as you can so you can try them out. See "Mechanical Tillage" on page 126 for more information on choosing and using a tiller.

HOW TO MAINTAIN: Clean all clinging soil off the body of the tiller after each use, especially vents and screens used for cooling. For more tips, see "Maintaining a Tiller" on page 123.

SOIL CARE FOR YOUR PLANTS

lants share common requirements for growth—
they all need light, water, oxygen, warmth,
support, and nutrients. But different types of
plants, and individual plants within those types, vary
in what those needs exactly are. Some tolerate heavier
soils than others, some demand more nutrients than
others, some withstand drought better than others.

To have the healthiest plants for the least amount
of work, you either have to choose plants that are right
for your soil or adjust the soil so it's right for the plants
you want. But choosing plants compatible with the
soil is just part of successful gardening. It's equally
important to choose plants adapted to your climate.

You can find information about adapted plants from
several sources. In most states, the Cooperative Extension Service publishes lists of suggested plants based
on research trials at the state's agricultural college.
A nearby botanical garden may also be able to advise
you about plants that are adapted to your area. Ask
questions at your garden center, and talk to your

neighbors to find out what grows well for them. Look
for gardening magazines that publish articles evaluating
plants for different climates.

Once you've chosen the best plants for your landscape, you'll need to know how to care for them. This
chapter covers the basics of soil care for common plant
groups. "Managing Vegetable and Herb Gardens" on
page 138 deals with soil preparation, fertilizing, and
mulching for these tasty crops; "Caring for Flower
Gardens" on page 142 covers these same basics for
your ornamentals. "Handling Trees, Shrubs, and
Vines" on page 146 explains the soil care needs of these
important landscape plants. "Growing Lawns and
Groundcovers" on page 148 takes the mystery out of
maintaining a great-looking lawn. To learn the basics
of producing good-tasting fruit in your backyard, see
"Feeding and Maintaining Fruiting Crops" on page
150. And if you enjoy growing plants indoors or
outdoors in pots, you'll definitely want to check out
"Caring for Containers and Houseplants" on page 152.

To get the most out of your garden, you can tailor your soil-care program to meet the needs of your particular plants.
Regular fertilizing, for instance, will encourage the best blooms from many flowering annuals.

Managing Vegetable and Herb Gardens

You can plunk a few tomato plants in a corner of your yard and get a few fruits for your trouble. But if you want to grow a variety of vegetables and herbs and get the best harvests you've ever had, it's definitely worth your while to prepare a good growing site and maintain the plants properly.

Preparing the Soil for Vegetables

In general, vegetables will thrive in normal, healthy garden soil with good drainage. Most grow best in a soil that is slightly acid or neutral (around 6.5 to 7.0). Vegetables that like the nutrient balance in alkaline soil include asparagus, melon, spinach, and Swiss chard. If your soil is too acid or alkaline, you may need to adjust the pH by adding lime or sulfur, as described in "Gardening in Acid Soil" on page 102 and "Growing in Alkaline Soil" on page 104.

Most vegetable crops will thrive in soils with a texture somewhere in the "loam" range: sandy loams, silt loams, and even clay loams. (See "Getting a Feel for Texture" on page 16 if you're not sure what texture your soil has.) Very loose, sandy soils with few rocks provide ideal conditions for root crops like carrots, beets, and parsnips. Celery and members of the cabbage family—like cauliflower, broccoli, and cabbage—can handle wetter soils that are more on the clayey side. Of course, working in ample amounts of organic matter can make almost any soil suitable for good vegetable production.

If you're starting a new site, strip off the existing sod, spread a 1-inch (2.5 cm) layer of compost over the area, and dig or till the top 6 to 8 inches (15 to 20 cm). (If you're not sure exactly when you should

Don't be tempted to skimp on spring soil preparation—it's the key to a healthy, high-yielding vegetable garden.

dig or what tool you should use, see "Cultivating the Soil," starting on page 117.) If you've planted an existing garden with a cover crop or green manure, dig or till it in at least 2 to 3 weeks before planting. Or, if you mulched the soil for winter, rake off the mulch or work it in to let the soil warm up. If you're growing root crops, make sure you dig the soil deeply and remove any rocks or clods that could impede good root development. Before planting, rake the soil to remove surface stones and clods and to form a smooth bed for seeds and transplants.

Mulch helps to keep the soil at an even temperature and moisture level, encouraging good root growth.

Fertilizing Vegetable Crops

Many gardeners have made a science out of fertilizing their vegetables, but it doesn't have to be terribly complicated. There are two approaches to fertilizing vegetables (well, three, if you count not fertilizing at all, which isn't very practical if you want good yields). The easiest method is to treat all your vegetables the same. Fertilize the vegetable garden each year, before planting, with a balanced material such as compost or a commercially available blend. For a midseason boost, side-dress with a dry fertilizer scratched lightly into the soil near the roots. Or instead of side-dressing, give all of the plants a monthly application of liquid seaweed or fish emulsion. (For more details on this technique, see "Applying Liquid Fertilizers" on page 84.)

The other approach is to fertilize each plant to meet its needs. This customized fertilizing is worth the trouble if

Drip irrigation is an easy and efficient way to make sure your crops get the water they need through the season.

Extra nitrogen will promote tender, succulent growth on leafy crops like lettuce, spinach, and collards.

Seaweed sprays provide trace elements and prevent deficiency symptoms, like black spots in beet roots.

you want to get extra-high yields or if you garden intensively (where the closely spaced plants need extra nutrients). To get the best results, you need to know which vegetables are heavy feeders and which aren't, and which need a little more of one nutrient than others.

Heavy Feeders Some crops, called heavy feeders, need a balance of nitrogen, phosphorus, and potassium, but in larger amounts than average or light feeders. Heavy feeders include members of the cabbage family (Cruciferae)—cabbage, mustard greens, broccoli, cauliflower, brussels sprouts, cress, and bok choy. Other heavy feeders are cucumbers and melons, which are in the squash family (Cucurbitaceae), and two members of the tomato family (Solanaceae): potatoes and eggplant. Asparagus, beets, corn, endive, lettuce, spinach, and Swiss chard are also on the list. Heavy feeders will benefit from lots of organic matter worked into the soil and used as a mulch. Or work in a green manure crop like vetch before planting heavy feeders. Also dig in an application of balanced fertilizer before planting. During the growing season, side-dress plants once or twice

When blossoms appear, spray peppers with Epsom salts (1 teaspoon to 1 gallon [4 l] of water) to add magnesium.

with more balanced fertilizer, or dose them with a spray or drench of seaweed extract or fish emulsion.

Light Feeders Some vegetable crops don't need high amounts of nutrients to produce good yields. Carrots, mustard, parsnips, peppers, radishes, and turnips are a few examples of light feeders. Soil-improving legume crops—including peas, beans, soybeans, and peanuts—also need few extra nutrients.

The organic matter you worked in before planting and the compost you use as a mulch will often provide all the nutrients these plants require. Of course, a light application of balanced dry fertilizer or liquid fertilizer during the growing season can help ensure plants are getting what they need.

Crops with Special Needs Some vegetables have more specific nutrient needs than just "more of everything." Cucurbits—melons, squash, and cucumbers—require adequate magnesium. Garlic, onions, squash, and tomatoes thrive with extra potassium and phosphorus but don't need much nitrogen. In fact, too much nitrogen will keep tomatoes from bearing fruit. If you want to make sure your plants will get just what they need, a soil test will be invaluable. That way, you'll know if your soil is deficient or adequately supplied with the necessary nutrients.

Soil Care for Herbs

In general, most herbs will thrive in average, well-drained soil. Adding some organic matter will keep the soil healthy and productive, but you don't need to add as much as you would for vegetables; herbs will grow just fine without the extra moisture and nutrients.

When planting, choose a spot with excellent drainage; most herbs (except the mints and a few

Rosemary grows best in light, well-drained soil; don't pamper it with compost.

To get the best from your tomato plants, hold off on the nitrogen—it promotes more leaves than fruit.

Onions, leeks, and garlic don't need much nitrogen, but they will grow best with extra potassium and phosphorus.

Rotating Vegetable Crops

Careful soil preparation and fertilizing doesn't do much good if an insect or soilborne disease routinely knocks out half your crop. Plants in the same botanical families often share the same insects and diseases. (For instance, tomatoes, peppers, and eggplants are in the family called Solanaceae; cabbage, broccoli, and cauliflower are in Cruciferae; and cucumber, squash, and melons are in Cucurbitaceae.) If you always grow the same plant or its relative in the same place, pests and pathogens will have an easy time finding their favorite food each season. But if you grow your crops in a different place each year, those troublesome problems may have a much harder time building up to damaging levels. If possible, wait at least 2, and preferably 4 or more, years before planting the same type of plant in the same bed.

Because soilborne diseases can travel—in rain, in soil clinging to tools, on your shoes—you can't plant a member of a disease-susceptible vegetable family right next to where you planted a relative the previous year.

You have to get some distance between the beds for rotation to stop diseases. A separate bed is ideal, but if that's not possible, opposite ends of a big garden will do. Rotations don't work well in small gardens.

Even if you don't have space for a disease-breaking rotation, your garden will still benefit if you carefully plan what goes where during different years. Growing a legume, such as bush beans, one year prepares the soil for a heavy nitrogen feeder (like corn) the next year. Alternate heavy feeders like cabbage and squash with light feeders like carrots and radishes, so the soil will have a chance to build up nutrient levels in between plantings of heavy feeders.

---

others) can't take "wet feet." If soil is naturally on the clayey side or if it's poorly drained, you may want to try double-digging (see "Double-digging for Great Plant Growth" on page 125) or building raised beds (see "Building Raised Beds" on page 100). Work in a 1- to 2-inch (2.5 to 5 cm) layer of compost or other organic matter at planting time.

After planting, you can supply most of your herbs' nutrient needs by mulching with ½ to 1 inch (1 to 2.5 cm) of compost. Make sure you don't pile the compost around the plant stems; many herbs are prone to root or crown

Mints spread quickly in moist soil that's rich in organic matter.

rot. (In fact, some herb gardeners surround the base of their herbs with a ½- to 1-inch [1 to 2.5 cm] thick layer of gravel to promote good drainage.) If you want to give your herbs a midseason nutrient boost, you can lightly and evenly scatter a dry balanced fertilizer over the soil surface and scratch it into the soil. Or spray herbs with a dose of liquid seaweed or fish emulsion.

Herbs growing in containers need a little extra care. Containers dry out quickly, so check them often. In hot weather, you may need to water every day. Each time you irrigate pot-grown herbs, nutrients wash out with the water that seeps from the bottom. Spray leaves every 2 weeks with diluted fish emulsion or compost tea to provide a steady supply of nutrients.

Potted herbs need more fertilizer as watering washes nutrients from the pot.

Well-prepared soil will support a wide variety of ornamental plants, including annuals, perennials, and shrubs.

Caring for Flower Gardens

To get beautiful flowers, you need strong, vigorous plants. To get strong, vigorous plants, you need healthy, fertile soil. Take good care of the soil, and your flowers will look better and be more prolific than ever. Of course, there are so many different kinds of flowering plants that it's difficult to provide general guidelines about their needs. Annuals, which live for only a season, require different treatment from perennials. And bulbs need a routine that differs from other perennials. Learning about the specific needs of your plants will help you supply the best possible growing conditions and get great results.

Preparing the Soil for Planting

As a broad generalization, flowering plants tend to thrive in a soil that is loamy and well drained, with lots of organic matter and a pH from slightly acid (around 6.0) to slightly alkaline (around 7.5). If your soil is on the sandy or clayey side, work in extra organic matter to provide the right growing conditions.

For annual and perennial flowers, double-digging the bed the first year will encourage good root production and vigorous growth for years to come. Double-digging, though laborious, loosens and improves the soil deeply, so roots can

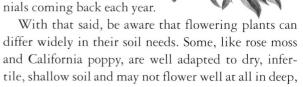

spread easily. It also breaks up any hardpan that might be slowing drainage and lets you add fertilizers and amendments farther into the soil profile than regular tilling does. (For more details on this technique, see "Double-digging for Great Plant Growth" on page 125.) In following years (for annuals), or if you don't want to bother with double-digging at all, turning the top 8 inches (20 cm) or so of soil is adequate.

It's also smart to take a soil test before you plant so you can correct any deficiencies. When you dig, mix in potassium, phosphorus, and any other fertilizers recommended in the soil test results. Or better yet, add them to your compost pile, then add the compost to the soil—the abundant, active microorganisms in the compost help break down rock powders and other low-solubility fertilizers faster than the smaller, less-active soil populations do. Potassium and phosphorus are especially important to encourage healthy roots that will keep perennials coming back each year.

With that said, be aware that flowering plants can differ widely in their soil needs. Some, like rose moss and California poppy, are well adapted to dry, infertile, shallow soil and may not flower well at all in deep,

Annuals are only in place for one growing season, so deep digging is not as critical for their success.

Perennials like daylilies and sea hollies *(Eryngium* spp.) can grow in the same place for years.

Potassium and phosphorus are especially important for good root growth and great-looking perennial flowers.

fertile conditions. Others, like astilbes and cardinal flowers, will turn brown and crispy unless they have rich, evenly moist soil. Either buy only plants that are adapted to the conditions your garden has to offer or be willing to put some work into creating the right conditions to fit the plants you want to grow.

To make compost tea, first tie a shovelful of compost in a burlap sack. Then soak it in water for several days.

You can find out the soil and moisture needs of flowering plants by looking in gardening books and magazines or by asking your local Cooperative Extension Service office or botanical garden.

Looking after Annuals

Annuals are the tourists of gardening; they show up when the weather turns nice but don't stay to tough out the winter. Their short stay means they don't have much time to extract slow-release fertilizers from the soil. Before planting, mix balanced fertilizer or compost into the soil to feed the microorganisms and provide a small, steady supply of nutrients to the annuals.

During the growing season, give annuals more readily available nutrients with a liquid fertilizer such as seaweed extract, fish emulsion, or compost tea. You

can spray the seaweed, emulsion, or diluted compost tea on the leaves, or drench the soil near the plant with it. A monthly application is plenty.

Some annuals, like annual aster (*Callistephus chinensis*), geraniums, impatiens, marigolds, petunias, and zinnias, may take a break from flowering when the weather gets hot. Don't give these plants extra fertilizer at this time; it can push them to grow when they need to rest. When the weather turns a little cooler and plants start to grow and flower again, you can start fertilizing again.

Give zinnias and other annuals a nutrient boost with a monthly dose of liquid fertilizer, like compost tea.

Delphiniums demand nutrient-rich soil and a steady supply of moisture. Mulching with compost helps meet both needs.

Caring for Perennials

Unlike annuals, perennials stay in the same place for years. Since you only have one chance (before planting) to get the soil into good shape, take time to prepare their beds well. As mentioned above, double-digging is a good way to promote strong, healthy plants.

After planting, add a thin layer of compost, well-rotted manure, dried grass clippings, or other fine-textured organic matter to the soil surface. Worms and other soil organisms will slowly work the material into the soil. If you wish, cover that layer with a coarse-textured mulch, such as bark nuggets or cocoa hulls, to conserve moisture, keep weeds down, and make the planting look more

polished. If slugs or snails are a problem in your area, you may want to keep mulches to a minimum to avoid encouraging these pests.

In cold climates, you may want to protect your perennials with a winter mulch. Don't put the mulch on until the soil has frozen. The point of a winter mulch isn't to keep the roots warm but rather to keep the soil evenly cold. Frozen soil won't shift around and heave plants out of the ground as will one that thaws and freezes. Carefully rake the mulch off as spring approaches so the soil can warm up faster. (Cool soils can slow plant growth in spring and encourage some diseases as well.) To learn more about choosing and using mulches, see "Making the Most of Mulch" on page 48 and "Organic Mulches," starting on page 52.

Once your perennials are established, you can't go back and dig in more soil-improving materials. But you can continue to top-dress the bed with fine-textured sources of organic matter, such as compost or grass clippings, raking back any mulch first. The finer the material, the faster it will decompose, so consider pressing it through a wire screen to crumble it into smaller bits.

Most perennials—all but the heavy feeders—will grow happily with this annual treatment. To meet

Nasturtiums grow best in average to poor soil; too much nitrogen will promote leaves instead of flowers.

An annual mulch of compost is all coreopsis (Coreopsis spp.) needs to produce strong stems and lots of flowers.

Give snapdragons soil with lots of organic matter, and they will repay you with a colorful show until frost.

the requirements of heavy feeders, or to encourage exceptional blooms from some of your other perennials (pinks [*Dianthus* spp.], lilies, and delphiniums, for instance), you may want to add some extra fertilizer. Push aside any mulch or compost first. Add phosphorus and potassium, as well as any other nutrient recommended in your soil test results. Apply them just as the plants begin setting flower buds. Scratch the fertilizer into the soil lightly with a hand cultivator, then replace the mulch.

Some perennials don't need, and indeed don't want, more fertilizer than a layer of compost. Sages (*Salvia* spp.) and coreopsis (*Coreopsis* spp.), for instance, become leggy and topple over with too much fertilizer. It's often hard to know how a given plant will respond to extra fertilizer. If a plant is looking stunted or isn't blooming much, you may want to try a supplemental feeding and see how it responds.

Growing Hardy Bulbs

With little care, hardy bulbs will come back to grace your garden year after year. Good drainage is critical for most bulbs; they are prone to rot in wet, oxygen-poor soil. If you are planting a whole bed, work in plenty of compost before setting in the bulbs. Or, if you're planting around perennials and shrubs or in the lawn, just dig a small hole for each individual bulb.

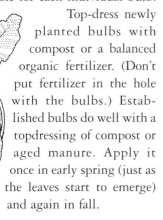

Top-dress newly planted bulbs with compost or a balanced organic fertilizer. (Don't put fertilizer in the hole with the bulbs.) Established bulbs do well with a topdressing of compost or aged manure. Apply it once in early spring (just as the leaves start to emerge) and again in fall.

If container-grown perennials dry out, immerse the pots in water.

To get the best growth and flowering for the least work, combine plants that have similar soil and fertility needs.

Handling Trees, Shrubs, and Vines

Trees, shrubs, and woody vines—known collectively as woody ornamentals—stay put for a long time. Put some extra care into preparing the planting area and getting the plants established; after that, they'll mostly take care of themselves with little help from you.

Mulching Woody Plants

A layer of organic mulch is an important part of meeting the needs of woody plants, as long as you apply it carefully. Mulch newly planted woody ornamentals with a ½- to 1-inch (1 to 2.5 cm) layer of compost, in a circle extending a foot or two (30 to 60 cm) beyond the farthest reach of the branches. Cover the compost with a 1- to 2-inch (2.5 to 5 cm) layer of a coarser mulch, like wood chips, to hold in moisture and keep weeds down. Keep all mulches several inches away from the trunk to avoid disease and rodent damage. Each spring, pull back the top layer of mulch, add more compost, and replace the mulch.

A spring application of balanced organic fertilizer or compost will keep your shrubs looking great.

Fertilizing Trees and Shrubs

After the first year or two, most woody plants have put out enough roots to search out the nutrients they need. But if your soil is naturally infertile (on the sandy side), or if you suspect that the plant may have a nutrient deficiency, you may want to give your trees, shrubs, and vines an extra shot of nutrients.

To effectively feed a tree, you really need to get the fertilizer down into the root zone. Poke holes in the soil that are a few inches (centimeters) across and about 4 to 6 inches (10 to 15 cm) deep.

Make a series of holes, 1 foot (30 cm) apart, in several concentric rings around the tree. The first ring should be far enough from the trunk that you won't gouge large support roots (probably a foot or two [30 to 60 cm]); the last ring should be right under the reach of the farthest branches (the drip line). Fill the

After they've been growing for a year or two, most trees will get along just fine without extra fertilizer.

Get young plants off to a good start with a layer of compost mulch; a midspring seaweed spray can help, too.

Mulch acid-loving plants like azaleas and rhododendrons with pine needles or chopped oak leaves.

Flowering shrubs may need extra potassium or phosphorus; add greensand or rock phosphate if blooms are scarce.

holes with compost or a balanced dry fertilizer. Don't fertilize after midsummer, or you'll encourage tender growth that winter kills easily. Fertilizing every 3 or 4 years should keep your tree in top shape.

Feeding shrubs and vines is easier. You can spray the leaves with liquid seaweed in midspring or spread a dry fertilizer or compost at the base of the plant in early- to mid-spring. Fertilize these smaller plants once a year to encourage good growth.

Get Them Off to a Good Start

Half of growing great-looking ornamentals is choosing plants that are naturally well adapted to your climate and growing conditions. The other half is planting the trees, shrubs, and vines properly to help them get established quickly and grow vigorously.

One mistake many gardeners make when meeting the soil needs of woody plants is to assume the roots are deeper than they are. While big support roots do go deep, the small roots that absorb water and nutrients are near the surface, and they spread out at least as far as the ends of the branches.

Below you'll find directions for planting a single tree or shrub. Whenever possible, though, consider creating larger planting areas, where you can plant several trees and shrubs together. They all will benefit by the extra rooting room.

1. Measure the depth and width of the plant's container or root ball. Then dig a hole as deep as the roots and twice as wide.

That way, the plant will have a base of firm soil to support it and the roots will have room to spread out.

2. If your plant is in a pot, slide it out or cut off the container. If you see roots circling around the outside of the soil ball, loosen them with your fingers or cut the circling roots with a knife.

3. Place the plant in the center of the hole. If your plant's roots are wrapped in burlap, remove the ropes, and cut off as much of the fabric as you can without jostling the roots.

4. Fill in around the roots with the soil that you removed from the hole. When the hole is almost full, pour in enough water to make mud, and wiggle the trunk gently to help eliminate any air pockets. Then fill in the rest of the hole and water again with fish emulsion, seaweed extract, or compost tea. Mulch with compost.

If you prepare the soil well before you plant and then mulch, your groundcovers won't need much attention.

Growing Lawns and Groundcovers

Lawn care has become something of a suburban art form. Mowing, weeding, watering, and fertilizing the lawn are the basic yard-care chores for millions of homeowners across America. Fortunately, you can enjoy a great-looking lawn without using any of the synthetic fertilizers or pesticides that are commonly sold for lawns. As with other plantings, a healthy, vigorous lawn starts with good soil care.

Planting a New Lawn

If you're beginning with a bare lot, start by having a soil test done. Then use a rotary tiller to loosen and smooth the soil. At the same time, work in a 1/2- to 1-inch (1 to 2.5 cm) layer of compost and any fertilizers or amendments the soil test told you the soil needed. Rake the area to remove weeds and clumps of old sod and to make a fine seedbed. To adjust the grade for drainage, use the back of the rake to move soil around. Then spread the seed and tamp it into the soil with the head of your rake or a lawn roller. Cover the area with a light straw mulch, and sprinkle it gently with water two or three times a day to keep it moist until the new grass pokes a few inches (centimeters) above the soil. Gradually cut back on watering. Avoid walking on or mowing the area until the grass has been up and growing for a few weeks and is at least 2 inches (5 cm) tall.

Renovating an Old Lawn

If you want to spruce up your existing yard, there are a few ways to go. If the area is very weedy and sick-looking, you may want to strip off the existing sod and start from scratch, as explained in "Planting a New Lawn." If there are just a few bad patches, you can just spot-treat them. Vigorously rake the area to loosen the soil and remove any thatch. Spread a thin layer of compost over the patch and rake it in until the area is smooth. Scatter seed evenly over the area, tamp it into the soil with the head of your rake, and cover with a light scattering of straw mulch. Keep the area moist until the seeds germinate. Wait a few weeks to mow the area.

Fertilizing Your Lawn

If you already have a healthy lawn, fertilizing can be as simple as just returning the clippings to the soil. Mulching mowers chop up grass clippings into tiny bits that easily decompose, steadily returning nutrients to the soil in small doses. You can

Aerating your lawn can discourage mosses from forming.

Some gardeners enjoy a casual-looking lawn; others would start over.

If part of your lawn is compacted by foot traffic, replace it with a path.

A smooth, green lawn does take some work, but it will form a beautiful backdrop for colorful flower gardens.

buy a mulching mower, or save money by buying an inexpensive blade to convert your current bagging mower to a mulching one.

If you've inherited a bedraggled lawn or want your healthy lawn to look superb, you may want to supply extra nutrients in some form of fertilizer. You can apply finished compost as a topdressing, or you may choose to use one of the commercially available organic lawn fertilizers. The best time to fertilize is when your lawn is going dormant (fall in the North and spring in the South). If your lawn is healthy, a single yearly application is fine. If you want to give a weak lawn an extra boost, you may want to fertilize twice a year.

If you're using compost as a topdressing, rub it through a screen first to break up the lumps. A thin layer—about $1/4$ inch (6 mm) thick—of compost will help vitalize the lawn without matting down the grass. If you are applying a commercial organic lawn fertilizer, check the label for suggested application rates; roughly 20 pounds (10 kg) per 1,000 square feet (93 sq m) is about average. A lawn spreader is a handy piece of equipment for applying most commercial fertilizers and screened compost. Over small areas, you can just scatter the fertilizer or compost by hand.

Aerating and Dethatching

Besides fertilizing and watering, some lawns also need aerating. Soils might be short on oxygen because frequent foot traffic has squashed the pore space out of them. Some soils just tend to be heavy and compacted. To loosen them up and promote better lawn growth, use an aerating device in the spring or fall, when the soil is actively growing. For more on using aerating devices, see the Lawn Aerator entry on page 134.

Thatch, though common on lawns overtreated with chemical fertilizers, sometimes develops on organically managed lawns, where there aren't enough soil micro-organisms to break down grass clippings. Thatch is a spongy layer of tan, partially decomposed grass blades between the living grass blades and the soil. Thatch makes it hard for roots to reach the soil and provides ideal conditions for many diseases.

If the thatch layer is more than $1/2$ inch (12 mm) thick, it's time to dethatch. Do it when the grass is actively growing, since vigorously growing grass will recover sooner. You can use either a dethatching rake or rent a power dethatcher. Once you've ripped out and raked off the thatch, spread a thin layer of fine compost on the soil to encourage microorganisms that will prevent the problem from recurring.

Soil Care for Groundcovers

Although you may just think of groundcovers as a substitute for grass, you should treat them more like a flowering perennial when establishing them. If practical, it's great to double dig the area; at the very least, loosen up the top layer and dig in organic matter, phosphorus, and potassium before planting. After planting, mulch with a thin layer of compost and then a coarse material to prevent erosion while the groundcover fills in.

Water Wisely

Watering, like fertilizing, is something of a national obsession. The general rule for lawn watering is to water infrequently and deeply. This advice works best for loamy soils. Fast-draining, sandy soils need more-frequent watering, but they take less water to moisten the root zone each time. Heavy, clayey soils will take more water, but you won't be able to apply it all in one session.

To see what works best for you, try irrigating for 30-minute intervals (on for 30 minutes, off for 30 minutes); if the water starts running off instead of soaking in, go with smaller intervals. If the water drains quickly into the soil, you can water for longer periods. Once the root zone is moist, you can probably wait at least a week or two before watering again.

Feeding and Maintaining Fruiting Crops

Many gardeners agree that there's nothing quite like the taste of home-grown fruit. With careful plant selection and good soil care, you can enjoy the pleasures of your own home orchard.

Choosing the Right Soil Conditions

In general, most fruiting plants prefer a deep, loamy soil that drains well, is slightly acid, and has a good supply of organic matter. Of course, there are some exceptions: Grapes, for instance, do best in a sandy soil, while blueberries require a very acidic soil.

Fortunately, many fruiting plants tolerate less than perfect soil and moderately acid soils with a pH around 5.5; the only thing most won't stand for is heavy clay. If heavy clay is all you have to offer, you have a couple of choices. You can build raised beds and—if growing fruit trees—plant dwarf cultivars.

Frequent sprays of fish emulsion will provide trace elements and can encourage good fruit set on your apple trees.

The other choice is to work generous doses of organic matter into the soil over an area big enough to accommodate the roots as the plant matures. Adding organic matter will help improve water and nutrient retention in sandy soils as well.

Preparing for Planting

Your fruit trees will live in one spot their whole lives, so make sure you put extra effort into preparing a good planting area. Remove the sod and, if possible, seed a green manure crop the year before you plan to plant, to suppress weeds and improve the soil. For planting guidelines for container-grown or balled-and-

In spring, treat your nut trees to a thin layer of compost mulch or a scattering of balanced organic fertilizer.

Avoid fertilizing fruit trees after midsummer; otherwise, you'll encourage tender growth that's prone to cold damage.

Blueberries are generally light feeders—a yearly layer of compost mulch is all they need.

burlapped plants, see "Get Them Off to a Good Start" on page 147. If you bought the plants by mail, they'll arrive bareroot. If you can't plant right away, keep the roots moist by surrounding them with wet peat moss. When you do plant, build a cone-shaped soil mound in the center of the planting hole and spread the roots out around the mound. The mound should be high enough that the plant is at the right height when you fill the hole with soil. Add a cup of bonemeal to the fill soil before returning it to the hole.

To know how deep to set a grafted plant, look for a lump at the base of the trunk or main stem; that's where the scion, or upper portion, was grafted onto the rootstock. If it's a dwarf or semidwarf tree, plant so that the graft union is about 2 inches (5 cm) above the soil surface. If it's a standard (full-sized) tree, the graft union goes an inch or two (2.5 to 5 cm) below the soil surface.

After planting, cover the soil with a 1- to 2-inch (2.5 to 5 cm) thick layer of compost, spreading it as far out as the ends of the branches. Then cover the compost with a woody, bulky mulch that decays slowly and suppresses weeds well—bark nuggets are ideal.

Fertilizing Fruits

For some fruits, a yearly layer of compost is enough fertilizer if the soil doesn't have nutrient deficiencies. These light feeders include blueberries, brambles, currants, figs, gooseberries, mulberries, and persimmons. For cherries and heavy-bearing plum trees, mix in a cup of a potassium source with the compost. If you notice deficiency symptoms, have a sample of leaves analyzed; this type of tissue analysis tells more about the problem than a soil test can.

Special Needs of Some Fruiting Crops

While all fruiting plants will respond to good general care, here are some special tips you can try to get the most from your crops.

- **Apples** Spray with fish emulsion just before the flower buds open. Afterward, spray leaves every 2 weeks through the summer to provide micronutrients. Follow soil test recommendations to keep potassium levels adequate.
- **Blueberries** Adjust soil pH to fall between 4.5 and 5.2 for best growth. Blueberries have shallow roots that are easy to damage if you cultivate around the plants for weeds; mulch deeply instead.
- **Grapes** Grapes are heavy feeders. Add colloidal phosphate to compost before applying it around vines. Test for potassium regularly and add as needed. Grapes grow best at a pH between 5.0 and 6.0.
- **Peaches and nectarines** These heavy feeders don't have extensive roots, so remove all sod in the root zone and keep plants mulched. Mix bonemeal or colloidal phosphate into the planting hole. Add potassium to the compost mulch. Spray leaves every 2 weeks through the summer to supply micronutrients.
- **Strawberries** Add compost to the bed before planting. Mulch regularly with compost and straw; apply an extra 2 to 3 inches (5 to 7.5 cm) of straw or pine needles in late fall to protect the crowns in winter. In late winter or early spring, watch for new growth beneath the mulch. Pull back the mulch when pale new leaves begin to grow.

A special container can be a focal point in the garden. Clay pots are particularly attractive and natural-looking.

Containers are a great way to keep invasive herbs like mint from spreading throughout the garden.

Caring for Containers and Houseplants

If you never seem to have enough room to grow all the plants you want, why not try container gardening? From annuals and vegetables to perennials, shrubs, and small trees, many plants will adapt just fine to life in a container. Indoors or outdoors, gardening in containers is a great way to make use of every inch of space.

Picking Plants for Containers

You can find enough plants adapted to outdoor container gardening to satisfy almost any gardening urge. Some vegetables, such as lettuce, radishes, onions, peppers, and cucumbers (with a trellis) are naturally well suited because they have small root systems. The same holds true for most herbs. For vegetable crops with larger root systems, such as tomatoes and squash, look for dwarf or compact cultivars that have been bred to grow in small areas. Many flowering plants also do well in containers, including popular annuals and bulbs. You can even grow cold-hardy shrubs and small trees in large containers. If you want to grow a shrub or tree that is not cold-hardy in your area, plant it in a large planter box outfitted with heavy-duty casters, and roll it indoors for the winter. For indoor growing, the main limitations

African violets are easy-to-grow houseplants.

are the amount of light and space you have available. Some plants, like many fruit trees, perennials, and bulbs, need a cold period for normal growth, so they often won't perform well indoors. But when you consider all the beautiful and exotic flowering and foliage plants that will thrive indoors, you can choose from a wide variety of plants for almost any spot. Try a few herb plants or radishes or lettuce in a sunny kitchen window; cacti, African violets, or tropical plants in the living room; and maybe even some vegetables on a warm, sunny porch.

If you are growing plants in large pots, it is easier to move them around if you place the pot on a wheeled platform.

Watering Methods for Container Plants

Set plants in a tray that will catch runoff from overhead watering.

For slow but steady irrigation, run a wick from the pot to a pan of water.

Watering Containers

To grow healthy plants in containers—whether outdoors or indoors—you have to keep a closer eye on watering than you do for in-ground gardens. That's because container-grown plants have a smaller soil mass to supply them with the water they need.

As a general rule of thumb, most container plants like to be evenly moist, not very wet or very dry. Often, the surface may look dry while the soil beneath is still moist. Stick your finger into the soil and wiggle it around a bit; if the soil below the surface feels dry, it's probably time to water again.

A tray or saucer can help trap excess water that runs through the soil. For outdoor containers that dry out quickly, keeping a shallow tray filled with water can help keep plants moist. In damp weather, or year-round for most indoor plants, make sure you dump out any water standing in the tray about 15 minutes after watering. Otherwise, the soil can become saturated and the roots will suffer from a lack of oxygen.

For plants growing outdoors in small pots, watering is usually a daily task; larger containers can usually go for 2 to 3 days between waterings. Hanging baskets may need watering two to three times a day. During hot, dry summer days, outdoor plants use more water. Indoors, plants can often go a week or two between waterings, depending on their needs and the type of potting mix they are growing in. Indoor plants usually need more frequent watering in the winter, when forced heat makes houses warm and dry.

The type of container you use also influences how often you have to water. Clay pots tend to dry out quickly, especially outdoors. Plastic pots can go longer between waterings and are better for plants that prefer steady soil moisture.

If you forget to water and the soil dries out, re-wetting the soil can be a problem. Try submerging the potted plant in a bucket that is half to two-thirds full of water, so the water level is over the top of the pot. Hold the pot under water until no more bubbles appear; then remove the plant and pot and set it aside to drain.

Hanging baskets can dry out quickly. You may have to water them three times a day when the weather is warm and sunny.

Plants trained into "standards" need a heavy pot that won't blow over.

With regular care, even the smallest space can support a beautiful and productive container garden.

Picking the Right Potting Mix

As with garden plants, container plants need a good growing medium. But while soil is just fine in the garden, it is a bad choice for plants in pots when used alone. The frequent watering demanded by container plants will cause most real soil to compact into a tight, brick-like mass (or if your garden soil is very sandy, it will dry out much too quickly in a container). The answer is to use a potting mix that is specially blended for plants in containers.

Like "ideal" garden soil, a potting mix that drains well but holds some water and nutrients will provide good growing conditions for a wide variety of plants. You can buy a variety of potting mixes at your local garden center. Those that contain some amount of real soil are called soil-based mixes. These tend to feel heavy, and they generally hold more water. Soil-less mixes usually contain peat moss and/or vermiculite to hold moisture. These mixes usually feel very light and can dry out more quickly.

When you are faced with a row of different products at the garden center, it can be hard to choose which one to buy. If you grow a lot of one kind of plant (cacti or African violets, for instance), you may want to try a mix formulated especially for that plant. In most cases, though, an all-purpose mix is fine. Buy a small bag and see how your plants grow in it.

Some gardeners get good results by purchasing a heavier mix and adding perlite or vermiculite to improve drainage or adding peat to improve water retention. "Make Your Own Potting Mixes" offers recipes for blending your own customized container growing medium.

Make Your Own Potting Mixes

If you want to give your plants the best growing mix for their needs, try blending your own. Make sure you mix the materials outdoors, or at least somewhere you can make a mess! A wheelbarrow or large bucket makes a handy mixing bowl, and a coffee can is a good measuring scoop; your measurements don't have to be precise. Mix the ingredients dry (you may want to wear a mask to avoid breathing the dust), and moisten the mix before you plant in it. Store unused mix in a container with a lid.

All-Purpose Mix

1 part commercial potting soil or good garden soil

1 part builder's (coarse) sand or perlite

1 part screened compost, leaf mold, or well-soaked peat moss

Cacti and Succulent Mix

1 part commercial potting soil, good garden soil, or screened compost (or half-and-half)

2 parts sand or perlite

1 part vermiculite

Moisture-lovers' Mix

1 part commercial potting soil or good garden soil

2 parts screened compost or leaf mold

1 part sand or perlite

Fertilizer Mix

(use 1 cup per 5 gallons of potting mix)

1 part bloodmeal

1 part rock phosphate, colloidal phosphate, or bonemeal

1 part greensand or granite meal

An all-purpose container mix will provide great growing conditions for a variety of potted flowers and shrubs.

Fertilizing Potted Plants

Even the best potting mix can't provide all the nutrients your container plants and houseplants need. To supplement, use a liquid fertilizer poured onto the soil. You can use fish emulsion, seaweed extract, or a combination of the two. Or make a nutrient tea out of compost, as explained in "Brew a Bucket of Compost Tea" on page 47.

For best growth, plan to feed your outdoor container plants each week. Houseplants vary in their appetites. Some people feed houseplants with very dilute fertilizers each time they water, some use regular strength with every other watering, and some feed monthly. Whichever routine you choose, remember to cut back or stop fertilizing during the winter, when low light slows growth.

Overfertilizing is as harmful as underfertilizing. An overfertilized plant produces weak, lanky growth that's susceptible to diseases and insects. And overfertilizing can make salts accumulate in the soil, creating conditions few roots like. The sure sign of salt buildup is a white crust on the soil surface or on the surface of clay pots. To get rid of it, pour water through the soil continuously (until water runs out the drain holes for several minutes) to wash out the salt. For severe problems, move the plant to a new pot or scrub the old one to remove the salt crust; wash the pot and repot the plant in fresh soil.

If you want to keep a plant in the same-sized pot, remove some of the old soil and replace it with fresh mix.

Repotting for Healthy Plants

If you plant annual flowers or vegetables in a container big enough to accommodate their mature size, they won't need repotting. But if you're growing perennials or houseplants, you'll eventually have to repot them.

There's no need to repot on a schedule; just watch your plant for signs that it's time. It's definitely time to repot when roots start growing from the pot's drainage holes. It might be time to repot when water comes out the bottom of the pot within seconds after you pour it on the top. To check, remove the plant from the pot. If the roots encircle the soil ball in a tight mass, you need to repot. If not, slip the plant back in. It's a good idea to check any newly purchased plants, since they are often pot-bound. Here's how to repot:

1. Remove the plant from the pot by placing your palm flat over the soil with the stem between your fingers, turning the pot over, and sliding out the plant. (If the plant doesn't slide out, loosen it by tapping the pot on the edge of a table or by running a dinner knife around the inner edge of the pot.) For a larger container, turn it on its side and gently ease the plant out.

2. Get a new pot slightly larger than the original one. Place pebbles or a bit of broken clay pot over the drainage holes to keep the soil from running out. Make sure you haven't blocked the holes.

3. Add some potting mix to the new pot and set the plant on top. The top of the soil mass should be about 1 inch (2.5 cm) below the rim of the pot. If needed, take out the plant and add or remove mix to get the right height.

4. Center the plant in the pot and fill around the sides with potting mix.

5. Gently press the soil around the plant with your fingers. Water the plant, then move it to a shady place for 3 or 4 days while it gets over transplant shock.

INDEX

The numbers in bold indicate main entries, and the numbers in italic indicate illustrations.

ACKNOWLEDGMENTS

Photo Credits

David Aldous: pages 55 (left), 58 (right), and 133 (left and right).

Heather Angel: opposite title page, pages 31 (top), 38 (right), 58 (left), 81 (top right), 107 (left), and 142 (bottom).

A–Z Botanical Collection: pages 62, 69 (left), and 144 (bottom).

Gillian Beckett: page 56 (right).

Bruce Coleman Ltd: page 12; photographer Jane Burton: pages 27 (top) and 81 (bottom left); photographer Robert P. Carr: page 61; photographer Eric Crichton: endpapers, contents page (bottom right), pages 32, 46 (top), 79 (right), 84, 113 (top), and 119 (top right); photographer Neville Fox-Davies: page 150 (bottom left); photographer Charlie Ott: page 151; photographer Prato: page 66 (left); and photographer Hans Reinhard: page 24.

Thomas Eltzroth: pages 21 (top), 28 (top), 109 (top), 110 (bottom), 140 (top), and 143 (bottom).

Derek Fell: back cover (top), contents page (left), pages 29, 35 (left), 42 (top), 50 (bottom), 108, 135 (right), and 138 (bottom).

Garden Picture Library: photographer Lynn Brotchie: page 154 (top); photographer Linda Burgess: page 42 (bottom); photographer Brian Carter: pages 51 (top right), 53 (right), 60 (bottom), 107 (right), and 147 (top left); photographer Bob Challinor: page 136; photographer John Glover: page 73 (right) and 150 (bottom right); photographer Marijke Heuff: page 72 (left); photographer Neil Holmes: page 78 (left), 118 (bottom) and 146 (top); photographer Michael Howes: pages 18 (bottom), 86, 127 (bottom left), and 140 (bottom right); photographer Roger Hyam: page 70; photographer Lamontagne: copyright page; photographer Jane Legate: page 81 (top left); photographer Clive Nichols: page 152 (top left); photographer Jerry Pavia: page 105; photographer Joanne Pavia: page 119 (top left); photographer J. S. Sira: pages 98 (top), 101 (top), and 154 (bottom); photographer Brigitte Thomas: pages 99 (top) and 126 (bottom); photographer Mel Watson: back cover (center), pages 20 (right), 49 (left), and 125; and photographer Steven Wooster: page 85 (bottom).

Gardener's Supply Co., Burlington VT: page 130 (left).

Grafton Agriculture Research Station: page 64 (left).

Harry Smith Collection: back cover (bottom), opposite contents page, pages 43, 48 (bottom), 56 (left), 57 (left), 59 (right), 68 (left), 76 (bottom), 96, 121 (bottom), 135 (left), 146 (bottom), and 148 (bottom right); photographers Smith/Polunin: pages 60 (top) and 65 (left).

Holt Studios: photographer Nigel Cattlin: half-title page, pages 16 (center left), 20 (left), 28 (bottom), 30 (top and bottom), 34 (right), 36 (right), 37 (right), 39 (right), 47, 63 (left and right), 66 (right), 69 (right), 74, 75 (bottom), 76 (top), 79 (left), 80 (top and bottom), 104 (bottom left), 114 (center), and 118 (top); photographer Jurgen Dielenschneider: page 16 (far left); photographer Michael Mayer: page 15 (top); photographer Rosemary Mayer: pages 111 (top) and 115 (top); and photographer Duncan Smith: page 127 (top).

International Photo Library: page 153.

Andrew Lawson: pages 54 (right), 113 (bottom), and 152 (top left).

Paul McDaniel: page 22 (far left, center right, and far right).

S & O Mathews: pages 44 (bottom right), 116, 143 (top left and top right), and 150 (top).

Peter May: page 114 (bottom).

New York State Agricultural Research Station: page 37 (left).

Clive Nichols: pages 44 (top), 82, 83 (right), 115 (bottom), 138 (top), and 139 (bottom).

Mark Norton: page 68 (right).

Papilio: pages 15 (bottom center), 31 (bottom), 33 (left and right), 34 (left), 35 (right), 39 (left), 48 (top left), 88 (left), and 92 (right).

Jerry Pavia: title page and page 152 (bottom).

Joanne Pavia: pages 59 (left), 127 (bottom right), and 139 (top).

Roger Pennock: pages 19 (center) and 22 (center left).

Photos Horticultural: pages 8, 17, 18 (top), 21 (bottom), 27 (bottom), 40, 44 (bottom left), 45, 48 (top right), 51 (top left), 55 (right), 64 (right), 67 (right), 73 (left), 75 (top), 77, 81 (bottom right), 83 (left), 85 (top), 90 (left), 98 (bottom), 99 (bottom), 100, 101 (bottom), 102 (top and bottom), 103 (top), 104 (top and bottom right), 106 (top and bottom), 109 (bottom), 110 (top), 111 (bottom left and bottom right), 112, 114 (top), 120, 122 (left and right), 124, 128, 129 (right), 131 (right), 132 (left and right), 134 (left and right), 140 (bottom left), 142 (top), 144 (top), 145 (top and bottom), 147 (top right), 148 (top, bottom left, and bottom center), 149, and 155.

Positive Images: photographer Jerry Howard: pages 16 (center right) and 57 (right).

Premaphotos Wildlife: photographer K. G. Preston-Mafham: pages 26, 36 (left), 38 (left), and 67 (left).

Rodale Stock Images: 15 (bottom left and bottom right), 16 (far right), 44 (bottom center), 46 (bottom), 50 (top), 54 (left), 65 (right), 72 (right), and 126 (top); photographer Mitch Mandel: pages 91 (right) and 93 (left and right); and photographer Kurt Wilson: pages 88 (right), 91 (left), and 94 (left and right).

Nelson Thurman: page 19 (left and right).

Weldon Russell: contents page (top right), 118 (center), 119 (bottom), and 121 (top); photographer Cheryl Maddocks: pages 87 (left), 92 (left), 95 (left and right), 129 (left), 130 (right), and 131 (left); and photographer David Wallace: pages 49 (right), 52, 53 (left), 78 (right), 87 (right), 89 (left and right), 90 (right), and 103 (bottom).